Making a Living

Sophie Rochester

Making a Living

How to Craft Your Business

Sophie Rochester

NICHOLAS BREALEY
PUBLISHING

London • Boston

First published in Great Britain in 2021 by Nicholas Brealey Publishing
An imprint of John Murray Press
A division of Hodder & Stoughton Ltd,
An Hachette UK company

1

Copyright © Sophie Rochester 2021

A CIP catalogue record for this title is available from the British Library

ISBN 978 1 529 39393 4
UK eBook ISBN 978 1 529 39395 8
US eBook ISBN 978 1 529 39396 5

Typeset by KnowledgeWorks Global Ltd.

Printed and bound by Great Britain by Clays Ltd, Elcograf S.p.A.

John Murray Press policy is to use papers that are natural, renewable and recyclable products
and made from wood grown in sustainable forests. The logging and manufacturing processes
are expected to conform to the environmental regulations of the country of origin.

Nicholas Brealey Publishing
John Murray Press
Carmelite House
50 Victoria Embankment
London EC4Y 0DZ

Nicholas Brealey Publishing
Hachette Book Group
Market Place Center, 53 State Street
Boston, MA 02109, USA

www.nicholasbrealey.com

In memory of my mother – the master of making

Contents

About the author

Sophie Rochester is the CEO and founder of Yodomo, a marketplace for artists, designer-makers and craftspeople to share their creative skills and create additional revenue streams for their businesses. She is an advocate of the power and benefits of making.

Yodomo is a UK-based social venture with a mission to grow participation in crafts to support wellbeing and sustainability. It was awarded Highly Commended, Arts & Culture at the Tech for Good Awards 2021 and was nominated for Seedrs 'Seedling of the Year' in 2019. Harper's BAZAAR has dubbed Yodomo *'best for aspiring artisans'* and now works with hundreds of makers and craftspeople.

Before setting up Yodomo, Sophie founded and ran The Literary Platform, which continues as part of Exeter University. Sophie worked for over two decades in digital, content strategy and publishing, working with 4th Estate, Good Technology, Pan Macmillan, Hachette, Penguin Random House, Nesta, British Council, Royal Society of Literature and more. She also founded the Fiction Uncovered Prize and co-founded The Writing Platform with Bath Spa University and Queensland University of Technology.

She is listed as a Top 10 British Council UK Creative Entrepreneur on *The Guardian* Professional h.Club 100 list and in the FutureBook 40: The Bookseller's definitive list of publishing innovators in the UK 2018. She has also been a Trustee for Arvon and Spread the Word.

Sophie has spoken globally on culture and technology, including at the *Convention on the Protection and Promotion of the Diversity of Cultural Expressions,* UNESCO Paris; for the British Council's *Crossing the River* initiative in Beijing, Shanghai and Hong Kong; and as a keynote speaker at the MIX Conference, Tools of Change New York, Frankfurt Book Fair, Bologna Book Fair, Editech Milan and the London Book Fair. She also regularly guest lectures across the UK at Goldsmiths

University, Exeter University, University of East Anglia, Birkbeck University, University of the Arts and London College of Fashion.

Her previous publications include 'The Publishing Landscape in China: New and Emerging Opportunities for British Writers' (Nesta, AHRC, 2015), 'The Impact of Digital Publishing on the Literary Market' (Tuebingen University, 2015) and 'Whose Book Is It Anyway?' (Goldsmiths University, 2017).

Acknowledgements

Making a Living could only have been written having heard the myriad of experiences of our community of makers and craftspeople in building their businesses. It has been a privilege to learn from these and to distil and share this insight.

This book would not have been possible without the following esteemed contributors to whom I am enormously grateful. Emily Birkett at Hemingway Design, Charlie Bradley Ross at Sustainable Fashion Warehouse, Julia Clarke, Deborah Carré and James Ducker at Carréducker, David Crump at Cockpit Arts, Ranjit Dhaliwal at Studio Ranj, Michelle Drew at Est.24, Emma Mapp at Mapp of London, Sarah Marks at Button Bag, Katie Mitchell at By-Me Katie, Tabara N'Diaye at La Basketry, artist Sophie Nathan, Samantha Razook at Curious Jane, Emma Sibley at London Terrariums, Lily Smith at ANNA, journalist and writer Katie Treggiden, Harriet Vine at Tatty Devine, Miranda West at Do Book Company and Eli Wisloska at Love & Salvage for their invaluable insight. Additional thanks to Dionne Griffith at ANNA money and Veronique AA Lapeyre at Craft Scotland and the Green Crafts Initiative, for their help in helping me secure such useful extracts for the finance and sustainability sections respectively.

The Making a Living Programme™ is a project borne out of the wide-ranging work of the Yodomo team and reflects our commitment to finding ways to share this knowledge with our wider community, intially during the lockdowns. Thank you to Isabella Mitchell and Eloise Wales for their help in distilling this knowledge so effectively, and notably to Sandy di Yu who deftly pulled together the many disparate content threads of our learnings into coherent channels for this project.

Thank you to Paul Fuller, who creates video and photographic content for Yodomo for his generosity in regularly sharing his top tips for DIY content creation to our community of makers, and Kathrin McCrea for her photography used in this book. Illustrations, unless otherwise credited, are original works by Rebecca Reeves.

The Yodomo team has learned so much from working with makers and small crafts businesses and we're appreciative of their spirit of community and collaboration. We are enormously grateful to Arts Council England, Mayor of London, Tower Hamlets and Hackney Creative Enterprise Zone for their support of our projects related to The Making a Living Programme.

Many thanks to Holly Bennion, Chloe West, Lily Bowden and Robert Tuesley Anderson at John Murray Hachette for their help in making the *Making a Living* book a reality and to Nick Davies for first encouraging me to nurture the seed of an idea. Thank you also to Lesley Thorne for helping me to shape the proposal.

I am indebted to my business mentors from whom I continue to learn so much - Scott McDonald, David Mansfield, Ross Sleight, Richard Townsend, Mark Goodson at Cambridge Social Ventures and Katrina Larkin at Fora, whose sage advice and encouragement is invaluable.

Last but not least, my gratitude to my ever-supportive family for cheering from the sidelines, and to my husband Ranjit Dhaliwal, for his trust, encouragement and patient endurance of the many breakfast meetings on anything and everything to do with the business of craft and projects designed to make a living.

Introduction

Starting a creative business has never been easier. Makers, craftspeople, artists, designers and others have many more ways today to reach customers directly, and sell to them directly.

You're here because you are considering launching your own business, or you've started to sell your handmade products or kits and the next step is to try to professionalize what has grown out of a hobby or side-hustle. You might be someone who has been practising your craft for a long time who wants to bring their business and revenues up to date with the myriad of opportunities that technology is now bringing to the industry.

Participation in crafts and making is exploding around the world. With more time at home and the growing evidence linking crafts and wellbeing, making is having a major mainstream resurgence. Your business is part of this revolution, and now is the time to grow your business within this exciting market.

This resurgence of interest in crafts and making is sparking a new wave of creative entrepreneurship, from at-home entrepreneurs looking to turn their handmade products into businesses, through to skilled craftspeople looking to turn their creative skills into workshops or courses. Your skills and techniques can be turned into monetizable formats, building on the commerce of your handmade crafts but also taking your skills and techniques to create learning content that can create additional revenue streams.

The Crafts Council, the UK's national charity for craft, launched its third major piece of research into the market for craft in 2020. The findings of *The Market for Craft Report* revealed 'that there is a growing new generation of younger craft consumers. Savvy buyers, they like collecting and know what they want.' The report concluded:

Craft is no longer a peripheral or isolated area of specialist interest: it is now firmly established in the mainstream. The growth in the public's desire for authenticity, for experiences, for ethical and sustainable consumption have helped fuel an interest in making and in handmade objects.

Online craft purchases have grown from 5% of buyers (332k people) in 2006 to 19% of buyers (3.2m people) in 2010 to 33% of buyers (10.3m people) in 2020.

Online craft purchases have surged as a result of platforms such as Etsy, which has seen huge growth in the number of crafts and maker sellers on their platform. In 2018, more than 2.1 million sellers were selling goods through the Etsy platform. By 2020, this figure had grown to 4.3 million sellers across 234 countries, with 90 per cent of these businesses selling crafts or handmade goods (*Source:* Statista). This exciting new market offers opportunities and challenges alike. How can you make your business stand out against the competition and where can you add uniqueness and value?

Where and why we work is changing with more and more people being offered at-home working options. There are also many more people choosing a portfolio career or even considering full career changes. The year 2020 saw record numbers of new businesses founded in the USA, UK, France, Germany and Japan, and technology is moving fast to create easy, off-the-shelf solutions to support small enterprises (*Source*: FT). How can your business benefit from this new range of technology solutions, and enable you to grow your business through the automation of tasks?

The growth of online shopping and the rise of conscious consumerism (buy local, buy small business, buy ethical, buy sustainable) are also creating new fertile ground for creative entrepreneurs, and the emergence of affordable and easy-to-use and stylish e-commerce platforms such as Shopify and Squarespace now means that the barriers to entry for a budding entrepreneur to set up a creative business online are coming down all the time.

This growing number of artisanal and other creative businesses is not just growing its profiles and businesses via Instagram and Facebook, but also developing audiences and sales through marketplaces such as Etsy, Not On The High Street, Folksy and Yodomo and online payment mechanisms such as PayPal and Shopify. These technology-led businesses are transforming the way in which this new wave of 'real world' offline maker businesses are now able to operate.

Given that so many barriers to entry for small businesses have been removed, there has never before been a time to really ask yourself, 'If not now, when?'

Of course, setting up any kind of business is not without its challenges. Four out of five UK businesses fail within their first year, and, according to ONS figures, only 42.4 per cent of businesses that were started in 2013 were still trading five years later (*Source*: SimplyBusiness). The surge in entrepreneurship also means that businesses have to work increasingly hard to get noticed.

For craftspeople and makers looking to develop their businesses today, they need to be digital content specialists, online marketers and e-commerce experts, whilst also finding the time to actually make and create the goods they are looking to sell.

Making a Living has been designed for you as a practical guide for creative entrepreneurs looking for advice and direction in making their dream creative businesses a reality.

For many makers making the shift from 'enthusiast' to 'professional', or from 'side-hustle' to 'company', can be challenging. Often the business of running a company – including its financial, marketing and fulfilment obligations – can eat up crucial making and product development time.

Advice in this book has been pooled from the experiences of numerous crafts and makers businesses, crafts organizations and more, and looks to distil practical advice and inspiring creative entrepreneurship stories to help new businesses get the best possible start and, crucially, avoid common pitfalls.

It has been carefully designed to help motivate budding entrepreneurs – that's you – to see that crafting a new creative business can be more than just a pipe dream and help get your new business off the ground.

We recognize that the world of business moves fast and that changes to legislation, social media platforms, software and more can change overnight. As a reader of this book you also have free access to The Making a Living Programme™ where you can deepen your learning, keep up to date with these ever-changing elements and join a like-minded global community of makers and craftspeople.

These additional business planning resources are available by joining the The Making a Living Programme https://yodomo.co/pages/making-a-living. We suggest joining as soon as you start reading the title as there might be templates that we refer to that you may want to access in sequence.

Right now you're probably feeling at best excited about the future, at worst overwhelmed at the prospect of the level of work that is involved with starting or growing your business. But this is a business book with a difference, as it's been carefully designed for creative entrepreneurs just like you. While covering off the small business essentials it also carries a host of expert advice and inspiration from leading craftspeople and makers who have been exactly where you are *right now* – nervously anticipating the next step.

Use *Making a Living* as a specialist guide to craft your own personal roadmap to launch and grow your creative business today. Take that first step forward now and simply read on.

Onwards!

1

Understanding Your Motivations

Making a Living is designed to help makers and craftspeople at any stage of their creative business development. You might be someone who has developed a handmade product and want to sell it for the first time; you might be a craftsperson who has honed your skills over many decades but has never contemplated selling your skills as a new revenue stream, or you might be an established artist who is looking to create a side line of more commercial products to sell alongside bespoke commissions. Whether it's a new business idea or contemplating a new revenue stream it always pays to stop, reflect and write some things down before setting off on a given pathway.

Personal motivations

Trying to get to the root of the 'why' of your plans will help you and your business over the long term, and help act as steer when having to make crucial decisions. The first 'why' to consider is your own personal motivations. This is a self-reflection exercise so one that you might want to do on your own and really get to the heart of what it is that really motivates you.

The calming benefits of making and crafting are well documented, and many people come to these creative activities for the first time because they are trying to get away from other stress points in their lives. One major consideration, especially if you're at the beginning of your maker business journey, is that by turning your creative hobby into a business you can often risk losing your love for it. When you're setting up you need to keep your eye on the end goal. If you're organized and set up ways to either automate or outsource the other range of tasks related to your business, then there is no reason why you can't continue to find time for making *and* growing the business.

One of the biggest challenges of starting a business is the financial implications, and if you're in full-time employment, then making the jump from side-hustle to start-up business can be daunting.

Many crafter-makers have told me that the craft they love to spend all their free time practising when working nine to five in an office becomes a chore when they trade it for money. Essentially, once the novelty of selling wears off – and it always does – profit becomes important.

The following seven findings below have emerged from many in-depth interviews that Sarah Marks has conducted with people who do and don't manage to make a living from running their own business.

Sarah Marks

Sarah Marks is co-founder of the successful crafts kits business Buttonbag, which has been running for over a decade. She is also a doctoral candidate at the School of Business and Management, Queen Mary University of London, where her current research explores the true cost of entrepreneurship on business owners. We asked her to share her insight into what crafters and makers realistically pay themselves, and her seven top tips to build a profitable craft business:

Crafters and makers often say they are not motivated by money, but Sarah's research shows that the people who persist, and extract the most enjoyment from their craft businesses, manage to pay themselves decently, too. This may seem obvious, but it all too often seems to get forgotten in the first excitement of selling your own wares.

The overwhelming evidence suggests that, once your passion or hobby becomes a business, you need to prioritize making money out of it.

The following seven findings below have emerged from many in-depth interviews that Sarah conducted with people who do and don't manage to make a living from running their own business:

1. *Price your labour fairly.* Put a monetary value on the labour needed to produce each item. Your retail selling price should be at least double this figure plus double the material cost. Why?

   Nobody wants to work for 50p an hour. This holds true, even if you don't actually 'need' the money.

   You may at some point want to employ other people to help you. The price of your product should include a living wage for the maker – whoever it is, or for an employee's help in selling, promoting or delivering your products.

   Don't forget that, if you sell the fruits of your labour substantially below the market rate, it can drive down the price and makes it harder for other artisans (who might have a family to support) to earn a sustainable income.

2. *Price your products high.* Crafter-makers who earn a living are usually at the high end of the market. Many have found they need to double, if not triple, their initial prices to make their business sustainable. They are often surprised by how easily customers accept higher prices. Their experience suggests that consumers cognitively ascribe greater value to higher-priced products.

3. *Demonstrate the value of your products.* Successful entrepreneurs find ways to demonstrate the inherent value in their wares or

services that justify the asking price. They do not rely on low prices to build market share.

4. *Set a monthly minimum income goal.* Successful entrepreneurs usually have an income goal in mind, that is often based on the minimum wage they would accept in salaried work. They work out how many products they need to sell per week to meet that goal, after all fixed costs – platform fees, market stall, monthly website costs. This sober realization frequently leads them to develop higher end services/products. Set a realistic path towards your income goal and track your progress.

5. *Think seasonally.* It is normal to make 60–90 per cent of your sales in the last three months of the year. No one crafts in the summer. This is especially true if your products are mostly bought as gifts for other people.

6. *Target people with disposable income.* Profitable crafter-makers get their services or products in front of people who have money to spend, and the inclination to spend it. This doesn't just mean the wealthy – think about timing, gift-buyers and holidaymakers. This is where crafts fairs, Etsy, the internet and the wholesale market kick in, helping you reach people beyond your own location.

7. *Wholesale or retail?* If you are interested in wholesale, you need to price your product high enough at the outset to be able to still make a profit yourself. Wholesale normally means you sell your product to a shop at 30–50 per cent below the retail price. Major chains will expect to buy something for around £7 that they sell at £20. Don't expect socially minded organizations such as public galleries, museum shops and charities to offer better terms; their retail arms have been set up to subsidize their main mission – not the other way round.

Sarah Marks' findings clearly demonstrate that there are careful considerations to make on how you might run your business as you're starting out. It's really important to reflect on your own personal lifestyle choices, as how you decide to proceed will depend on your own personal situation, your finances and, importantly, your own approach to risk.

THE HOBBY

The link between crafts and wellbeing is well documented, and making with your hands has strong links to improved mood. One common perception is that by leaving your full-time job and turning your hobby into a business, you will suddenly have much more time for making and a freer lifestyle. In this instance, it's really important to keep in mind that running a full-time business will not necessarily mean *more* time for making or crafting, and that in order to run your business successfully much more of your time will need to be spent on content creation, digital marketing, business development, raising finance and more.

Keeping your full-time job and selling crafts or handmade items simply as a hobby might actually equate to exactly the same amount of time left for creativity, so it's important to really understand the extent of that other work before you hand in your notice.

Exercise

1. Ask yourself the difficult questions and get to the 'why' of you wanting to sell your work or skills commercially as opposed to just making and crafting as a hobby.
2. Are you seeking validation for your work?
3. Are there other ways to get your work validated other than turning your hobby into a business?
4. Are you drawn to the lifestyle of being a maker or craftsperson?

THE SIDE-HUSTLE

Having a side-hustle at work used to be something that was kept a little bit under the radar from employers, but today many more companies are actively encouraging side-hustles and consider it an asset if employees can think entrepreneurially. This is evidenced in intrapreneurship programmes, with the most famous example being that in the early days Google would actively encourage employees to pursue their side projects 'to inspire innovation in participating employees and ultimately increase company potential'.

Changes in the way that we work mean that running two, three or more different careers simultaneously is becoming more and more commonplace, and these portfolio careers create time and space to run businesses on the side and watch them grow, before having to give up other paid employment.

One major consideration for crafts and making businesses is the cyclical nature of sales across the year. For many businesses, sales of finished goods, kits and learning workshops centre around Christmas, and, as Sarah Marks' research above demonstrates, many businesses find that 60–90 per cent sales come in the lead-up to and during Christmas. This might be where a portfolio career might really give you an advantage.

Exercise

Use these three questions to map out a typical week, month and year to try to understand how much time you have to commit to a side-hustle business.

1. What are the implications of running two or more career paths simultaneously?
2. Have you left any downtime in between your multiple professional roles to support personal wellbeing?
3. Do your other roles sometimes seep into extra days – will you feel quickly overwhelmed or frustrated when you can't find the hours to launch your side-hustle properly?

THE FULL PLUNGE

For some people, it is all or nothing. In order to get an idea off the ground, it is going to require a singular focus and no distractions. However, before you hand in your notice to your employer, ensure that you've made a plan of action, especially around your financial viability in that crucial period as you are building your business.

Emma Mapp

Emma Mapp is a designer and a photographer who specializes in cyanotypes which she teaches through workshops and kits. She was a City of London lawyer before leaving her full-time job and returning to her love of photography and specialist photographic techniques. Here Emma gives her advice on what to consider before leaving the day job:

1. *Do your research.* Who are your competitors? Is there room in the market for your business? What is your contingency plan if your business plan does not succeed? Talk to other business owners and ask for their advice.
2. *Get into the habit of recording your finances* and think carefully about what you spend your money on. It's vital to keep an accurate record of your profit and loss – money is the life blood of a business, and it's important to have a comfortable relationship with it. You have to be able to make a living!
3. *Consider a collaboration or outsource.* Two heads are better than one, and it's impossible to be good at everything (IT, marketing, etc.). Think about collaborating with another person who complements your business but has different skills to bring to the party.
4. *Network a lot and get a mentor.* I found seeing a careers coach was an invaluable experience, and it enabled me to have the courage to set up my business ventures.

There's never a right or wrong time to start a business and other people will always have an opinion on whether you are taking a risk or not. If you have done your research and you have put a plan in place, then go for it! Be prepared to learn from your mistakes and successes.

When you're speaking to anyone who has left their job to pursue a new craft or making business, be sure that you understand their personal circumstances first as you might find, for example, that their financial situation is very different from your own. Be mindful that some business owners will normally readily share only the good news, and that you may not be getting the full picture on Instagram. Speak to craftspeople and makers who you can really trust to give you a rounded view of what it's really like to be running your own business before you make any big decisions.

Exercise

Use these questions to help you consider your own personal financial situation:

1. Can you finance the first year of your business even if sales are very low?
2. Are there specific upfront costs involved with your crafts or making business (e.g. kiln, specialist tools, etc.)?
3. What do you need to earn to cover your living expenses?
4. How long will it take to reach the point where your new business is covering your living expenses?

Purpose

The concept of 'purpose' in business is one that has been growing in importance in recent decades. Social enterprises and charities have long stated their mission, vision and values to their stakeholders, which then become an accountable set of standards to ensure that all activity serves those standards. This sense of accountability has seeped into the broader for-profit business world today with the growth of new business classifications, such as 'B-Corp', that encourage companies to be clear on their mission or purpose, and to ensure that business growth is not just serving its shareholders but also the planet.

In a 2009 TED Talk called 'How Great Leaders Inspire Action' (https://www.ted.com/talks/simon_sinek_how_great_leaders_inspire_action), author Simon Sinek introduced his Golden Circle theory, to help business leaders communicate the 'why' of what they do (Figure 1.1).

The Golden Circle

WHAT:
Every organisation on the planet knows what they do. These are the products or services they sell.

HOW:
Some organisations know how they do it. These are the things that make them special or set them apart from their competition.

WHY:
Very few organisations know why they do what they do. Why is not about making money. That's a result. Why is a purpose, cause or belief. It's the reason your organisation exists.

Figure 1.1 The Golden Circle (courtesy of Simon Sinek, www.simonsinek.com)

The Golden Circle exercise is a great way for entrepreneurs to get to the 'why' of what they do.

Exercise

- *Define the 'What?'* – What are the products or services that you intend to sell?
- *Define the 'How?'* – How will you sell your products or services, and how will you set yourself apart from your competitors?
- *Define the 'Why?'* – This is the most important part of your business, and sometimes gets overlooked – why are you doing what you do? What is the reason that your business exists?

You can also do your own research on the businesses that you admire and check out their mission statements. Here are some sample mission statements from bigger brands to get you started:

- *Ikea:* 'To create a better everyday life for the many people.'
- *Patagonia:* 'We're in business to save our home planet.'
- *Google:* 'To organize the world's information and make it universally accessible and useful.'

As a new business, it might feel a bit strange to be looking at these big-brand mission statements and writing your own. Getting to the 'why' of what you are doing, however, is an important exercise for any business at any stage of its growth, and will help you in making major decisions along the way. By having a clear idea of your purpose or mission, however, you will be better equipped to articulate your passion to your customers and all other stakeholders in your business. It will also help you think about what kind of a business you want to build.

As an important note, you may want to keep revisiting your mission statement as your business develops, and changes in personal circumstances may mean that your personal motivations evolve. It is unlikely that you'll easily get to a mission statement in a day, but by getting *something* down on paper initially, and revisiting this as you build and hone your business, you should start to see your true mission emerging, and this will help you anchor everything else you do as you grow.

Exercise

1. Consider your own personal motivations and financial situation, before deciding what kind of business you want to create.
2. Get to the 'why' of what you want your business to do and find your purpose.
3. Write a clear purpose or mission statement to ensure that you have a 'true north' pathway to guide you to success.

Once you have considered the 'why' and purpose of your new business, you will be ready to start thinking about the next steps to solidifying your offer and launching your business.

Let's get started.

2

Getting Started

The journey to starting a craft or maker business is often organic. You may have started to sell some handmade products to friends and family and just started taking payments online into your personal account. You may have been experimenting with making things and are looking to see if there is a market for these products. For more established crafts business owners, it might be that you have been creating very high-end gallery pieces and the prospect of creating a new product line to reach different commercial audiences, or just selling online, feels like starting a completely new business.

Whatever journey got you to this stage, researching and validating your business idea, and writing a business plan, are critical exercises to help you avoid common pitfalls.

Writing a business plan

Writing a business plan is a great exercise in helping you to communicate your vision, your goals and your financial plan. Business plans are often required by banks if you are looking for a small business loan, or by investors if you are looking for external investors. It is also a useful exercise at any stage of your business development, even if you are not looking for external finance, and will help you to shape the business and consider your plans carefully. The framework of a good business plan encourages you to consider all eventualities and helps you to consolidate your business goals and your vision for the future, helping you to communicate your vision, your goal, your products, your target market and marketing plan, your current financial state and your forecasts for the future.

Like many aspects of growing a business, your business plan will be founded on a number of assumptions, and your plans may change as your business evolves. The exercise of writing an initial business plan is to help you clarify what you are going to sell, who you are going to sell it to and how (e.g. online via e-commerce, in person at markets, etc.), and identify your vision for the business as it grows, and be able to envisage this and communicate it to others.

Exercise

Plot a first-draft business plan, writing a paragraph for each of the sections shown in Figure 2.1.

If you want to see some sample business plan templates, these are downloadable in The Making a Living Programme (https://yodomo.co/pages/making-a-living).

Remember that your business plan will be honed as you grow, so don't worry if there are some gaps in your draft plan – just plot what you can at this stage.

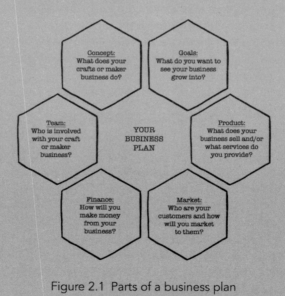

Figure 2.1 Parts of a business plan

What does your crafts and maker business do?

Before you get excited about what to call your new company or what the branding is going to look like, research your business idea and test out what you are proposing to sell with existing or potential customers. The most effective way to do this is to simply get out and ask people.

For early-stage businesses, this process can be challenging because you might only have a small number of – or no – customers to glean feedback from. In this situation, you may need to enlist the help of your family and friends and their extended networks, and ask them to give honest opinions on the things you intend to make. Consider who in your network can give the most insightful feedback. Do you have friends or family who work in relevant industries, or who understand any part of your business cycle – for example product development, retail or distribution, public relations (PR) or marketing? If so, enlist this group for feedback and hone your ideas before you launch.

If you have an engaged Instagram following, this is also a useful place to get quick feedback. Use Instagram Stories to ask your community whether they prefer a specific style, colour or form, for example. You can also use Instagram's stickers to survey your followers and ask questions that require a simple 'yes/no' response, or ask them to respond to specific questions with a written answer in order to glean yet more information. Your questions can be around your specific product (e.g. a preference in colour or range), or you can ask broader questions such as 'Is sustainable packaging important to you?' Even with small datasets from these questions, you can start to build up interesting pictures and see themes in responses.

You will often get conflicting feedback or advice, so remember that you are the decision maker and only you have final sign off on the shape of your business. Find a way to collate and prioritize feedback to help you shape your business, but also don't let one negative naysayer put you off an idea altogether.

What do you want to make and what other 'making' services could you offer?

While you might be focusing on one single product currently, try to anticipate how this might evolve over time. For example, if you create macramé plant hangers now, then consider how this might expand into other macramé products, or possibly more broadly into a textiles-led business.

If you're a craftsperson or maker, then the most obvious thing to sell is your finished product – the things you have made. However, you might also want to explore other associated revenue streams attached to your specific making skills and techniques. Can you teach workshops for children, for friends or events for major corporate companies? Could you create an online course that can sell in the background as you're making new products or product lines? Could you create a kit of materials and a printed guide to sell if people are more interested in learning how to make something than buying a finished product?

This big picture approach will also help you when you come to the crucial stage of naming your business and the branding associated with it. You should consider adding some flexibility to your company name and branding if you are thinking of ever branching out in the future, and not restrict the business with a name that dates quickly, or ends up describing only a small part of your eventual business.

While you're honing the proposition, this is also the point at which you should check whether there are any restrictions to your products. For example, there are much stricter regulations around selling products to children than there are to adults. A way to quickly understand which products might be prohibited is to read any guidelines provided by the bigger craft marketplaces.

For example, Etsy has a useful page at https://www.etsy.com/uk/legal/prohibited which explains its policy on what can, and cannot, be sold in its marketplace. Some products are more complicated than others, so you might want to avoid some products at launch which you could still introduce later on. Note that different countries will also have different legislation around product restrictions, so always consider this when you are looking at selling your products abroad.

Choosing a company name

If you decide to work under your own name, you will be saving a lot of time and decision making for branding your company. If you share your name with a celebrity or another business, however, it is worth considering how SEO (search engine optimization) might struggle to find your business on the first pages.

In this instance you might choose instead to use wordplay on your name to come to an original company name. For example, Claire Whelan is a UK-based weaver, and she trades under the name Whelan's Weaving. Carréducker is an artisanal shoe-making business in London and is an amalgamation of the partners' names, Deborah Carré and James Ducker.

Other inspiration for your company name might come from where you live – for example, Hanbury Press is the name of a bookbinder who started out on Hanbury Street, London.

You might also want to consider the following practicalities:

- Ensure that your new company name *doesn't have any inappropriate or offensive meanings* in another language, especially if you plan to have international customers.

- Consider where your new company name sits *alphabetically*. At Yodomo, we hadn't realized the significance of having a company name starting with the letter 'y' and so often get lost on a page that requires scrolling.

- *Typography*: some letters and alliteration lend themselves better than others to playful typography and branding.

Finally, check your name is *not being used by anyone else*. Some useful searches can help you establish this including:

- *Trademark search internationally:* establish quickly if anyone is trading under the same name. If the company is working in a very different sector to you, it may be possible to hang on to your name idea, but broadly speaking you shouldn't trade under the same name as a trademarked company.

- *Social media:* even if not trademarked, you should look to see if anyone is working under that name on social media.

- *Domain name search:* check to see if your company name is coming up in searches on a popular domain name registration site.

If you decide to incorporate your company and become a limited company or corporation, then your company name should end in 'Limited', or 'Ltd', or if your company is registered in Wales, then you would use the Welsh equivalents 'Cyfyngedig', or 'Cyf'.

In the UK you would register your company name with Companies House, which recommends that your company name does not contain any sensitive words or expressions, cannot be offensive, and does not suggest a connection with government or local authorities without express permission.

These same guides would apply to a sole trader (UK). Moreover, as a sole trader you cannot add 'Ltd' if you haven't registered your company with Companies House. You may also have heard the expression 'trading as'. A 'trading as' or trading name can be used by a sole trader, partnership or limited company to differentiate itself from its own name or a registered name. It can offer you a bit of flexibility if you want to operate under a different name to your personal name.

Domain registration of your company

Once you have settled on your company name, you can move on to the next step: securing your own domain name.

Your **domain name** is the website address that you will use across your website, in social media profiles, on printed materials and more, so it's important to get it right.

As mentioned earlier, you can easily check to see whether your chosen company name is already registered elsewhere with a trademark. However, when it comes to domain name registration, this can be a bit more complicated as you will realize that every seemingly thinkable combination of words has been registered already as a domain name. If you ever wondered why there were some vowel-dodging start-up names like Scribd, instead of Scribed, or Vestd instead of Vested, then this is why.

To keep up with the huge number of domain name registrations, you'll see that registration companies have brought in a range of additional domain name extensions such as .co .london .studio and more. These are handy if you really do have your heart set on a particular domain name, as you might find some availability with one of these new domain name extensions. However, you should think carefully if you can see another company operating under the same domain name but as a .com .co.uk and so on, as it can become confusing to the customer when trying to find you. What's more, if this other company is trademarked, then you may not be able to operate under that same name even with a different URL. Ideally, you want to find a domain name where you can buy the .com or, for UK readers, the .co.uk, and then you can choose additional options after that.

For example, let's say your company name is Cynthia's Ceramics and you want to have the domain name *cynthiaceramics.studio*. The *.studio* domain extension looks great and has a nice maker feel to it, but even if that is your chosen domain name, you might want to secure *cynthiaceramics.com* and *cynthiaceramics.co.uk* just to be sure that no one else buys these domain names and confuses future customers.

While you are searching for your domain name, you want to simultaneously check that the accompanying social media **handle**, or name that will be associated with your brand is also available.

The handle is how your brand will be discovered, tagged and recognized. It is essentially your username, and on most social media platforms it follows the @ symbol. You can check whether it's taken by doing a search on the platform in question. When you've settled on a handle you're happy with, you can start creating your accounts, and we go into more detail on setting these up in Chapter 8: Managing Your Accounts and Tax.

Registering your business

Once you have decided on your company name, you need to decide on the legal entity that your business will take. There are a number of different choices depending on the size of your business, whether you're working on your own or with other people, and depending on how likely you are to use VAT-registered suppliers.

The main categories of business registration are:

- *sole trader / sole proprietorship*: exclusive ownership of a business, liable for losses;
- *limited company*: a private company whose owners are legally responsible for its debts only to the extent of the amount of capital they invested;
- *limited liability partnership*: a separate legal entity from its members (partners), who are liable only for the amount of money they invest,

plus any personal guarantees. The partnership is incorporated and can be used only by profit-making businesses;

- *partnerships*: an association of two or more people as partners, who share management and profits of business.

REGISTERING AS A SOLE TRADER

If you're operating on your own, then the simplest option is to set yourself up as a sole trader. The advantages of being a sole trader are that there are very few set-up costs and you don't have to publicly share your accounts with Companies House. If you're still at the beginning of your small business journey, then being a sole trader gives you flexibility, and if you decide that you want to go back to full-time employment then the process is very straightforward.

The disadvantages of being a sole trader are that you are fully liable for any debts incurred by the company, and you may find that if you want to secure finance (bank loans etc.) that this is harder to do.

As a sole trader your paperwork will be lighter, but you will be required to do a self-assessment of your earnings each year.

REGISTERING AS A LIMITED COMPANY (UK)

A limited company (UK) is when the company has a legal identity of its own, which means that it is the company, not you as an individual, that enters into contracts, takes out business loans, and so on. You might also hear this referred to as 'incorporated' companies.

The advantage of being incorporated is that there is a clear distinction between 'the business' and 'the individual', so, if there are any problems in the future with, for example, finances, it is the business that is liable and not you. This means that as a limited company you would never be asked to use your own personal assets (such as your home) to repay any debts owed by the company.

What this also means is that any money coming into the business belongs to the business, so you would need to be clear about monies coming to you out of the business, whether this is as a salary or a dividend (a payment that is made to you if there are enough profits in your business).

Continuing with our example of Amy's Crafts. If this was a limited company – Amy's Crafts Ltd –you would become the sole director and shareholder and pay yourself either a salary or dividend from the company.

If you are personally paying out for expenses such as crafts materials, marketing costs and so forth, these would be repaid to you from the business. Becoming a limited company does create a few additional bits of paperwork, but long term it does protect your personal assets from being seized in the event of any financial issues. It would also open you up to other business opportunities such as bank loans, grants or investment that may not be available to sole traders.

We've already discussed naming your business above, and by becoming a limited company and registering your business's legal name at Companies House you are afforded some protection from duplication, while as a sole trader someone might register the same company name as you without any recourse available to you.

Registering your company at Companies House also acts as a 'trust signal' to your customers, something which is important to consider when you start a new crafts business.

If you are planning on working for corporates (see later chapters on developing a crafts workshop for corporates), you may find that they will work only with incorporated companies as part of their risk management strategy.

Depending on where you live in the world, there may also be attractive tax implications for being an incorporated company rather than a sole trader. See our links to further information at the end of this chapter to ensure that you're getting the advice you need relevant to where you live.

COMPANY INCORPORATION

Incorporated companies in the UK will be required to complete detailed paperwork each quarter (especially if registered for VAT) and each financial year, including filing accounts, annual returns and corporation tax returns. As an incorporated business you may find that it is better to invest in an accountant who can handle this paperwork for you, rather than you struggling to get it done yourself.

Many makers and craftspeople find accounting complicated, but there are a number of sophisticated accounting software packages that can really help small creative businesses, such as Xero and QuickBooks. These packages can help you keep track of your finances, issue invoices and more, and there are often detailed free onboarding courses to help you understand how to use the accounting tools.

If you're really uncomfortable with the terminology of finance and accounting, invest some time in just understanding the basics as it will really help you in your journey over the long term.

PARTNERSHIPS

If you want to go into business with another person, then there are several ways you can register your business as a partnership. The advantages of working with a partner are that you can share the burden or work and grow more quickly. Starting a new business can be daunting, and sharing the responsibilities involved can help to keep you motivated. Your business partner may also have a different skillset to yours. The downside is that you will have to share decision making around the business's direction, and sometimes this can be a challenge.

Partnership case study: Carréducker

Carréducker, founded by Deborah Carré and James Ducker, are bespoke handsewn shoemakers in London. They completed traditional shoemaking apprenticeships and worked independently for a few years, before founding initially as a limited liability partnership (LLP) and later as a limited company.

Their award-winning work features in the permanent exhibition at the Design Museum, London, and has appeared in shows at the Royal Academy, Somerset House and Buckingham Palace. The duo has grown a loyal global customer base and delivers the bespoke shoe service at Gieves & Hawkes in London, as well as services from their own bespoke atelier. Here Deborah and James share their top tips on running a successful partnership:

- Write down your vision for the business together and keep checking in over the years that you still share that same vision. Write a business plan with a one-year and a five-year time frame.
- Agree on a company structure before you start and be prepared to review it as your business develops.
- Accept that you are unlikely to make money for the first few years and that you may need to balance other work in order to survive financially.
- Trust is essential. *You* are the business, so every mistake is a shared mistake and every success is a shared success.
- Be aware of and discuss your own personality traits before you go into business together.
- Assess your strengths and weaknesses and play to your strengths.
- Find a fair way to work, agreeing on the working day, time commitment, areas of responsibility and so on.
- Accept that things change and that you and your business will need to adapt and evolve.
- Check in with each other every day to stay on track, especially if you work remotely.
- Talk to each other about work and home life – understand where the other person is coming from both from an empathetic and business performance perspective.
- Listen to your partner and be respectful of one another's viewpoint.
- Agree how you will get beyond any disagreements. Write an exit strategy in case things go wrong.
- If you make a mistake or do something wrong, say sorry; even if you're not in the wrong, say sorry and move on.
- Pick your battles and don't sweat the small stuff.
- Celebrate your successes together. Enjoy a win, an award, a big sale, a new order – these things keep you going through the lows.

There are several ways to structure a partnership, and you should refer to local legislation to establish the most appropriate for your business. 'Ordinary' partnerships are designed so that the business dissolves if one person leaves, whereas limited partnerships allow you to structure your business so that each partner is liable for the investment they've personally made.

If your work has a social, charitable or community-based objective to it, there are additional options open to you. You could still operate your business as a sole trader, limited company or partnership, but you could also set up a charity, a CIC (community interest group) or a cooperative. For UK businesses there is a lot more information on these at https://www.gov.uk/set-up-a-social-enterprise. We also explore the new socially responsible B-Corp movement in Chapter 13: How to be a Responsible Business.

The way you incorporate a business will always differ depending on where you live in the world. Always check online and ensure that you are following the most up-to-date information. These useful links below will help you with more local information on how to register your business, depending on where you live in the world.

Useful inks

UK

https://www.gov.uk/browse/business
https://www.gov.uk/set-up-business-partnership/register-partnership-with-hmrc

USA (information by state)

https://www.usa-corporate.com/new-business-resources/information-by-state/

Canada

https://www.ic.gc.ca/eic/site/cd-dgc.nsf/eng/cs06642.html

Once you've done some initial business planning and considered the best company structure for your business, the next step is to begin researching your ideal customers and research where you will find them.

3

Understanding Your Customers

As a new crafts and maker business owner, one of the most important things to do is to really start to understand who your customers are. You might think that you don't have a 'customer type', but you may start to see some themes emerging and this will help you consider what product lines to create, what price to set products at, and where to sell your products. For some businesses they might have one customer type for their finished handmade goods and a completely different customer type for their live workshops.

Large companies will work with swathes of data to help them to create detailed 'personas' for their customers. A persona is a way to try and visualize a customer type and consider what their daily habits are in order for companies to consider how best to target them. As a new, small creative business you may not have many customers at the beginning, nor much information about them. A good way to mitigate this at the beginning is to work with *assumptions* or *hypotheses* about your customers and then to challenge these with 'actual' data as you grow.

You can try to visualize who you *think* your customers are first of all, and then you can cross-reference with e-commerce sales data, or with what you can learn about your customers when you see them at crafts markets, for example. As your first-hand knowledge of your customers grows, you can check to see whether your original assumptions were correct and adjust your personas accordingly.

For example, when Yodomo first started trading, the team initially thought that its main audience would be 'millennials based in urban areas' and created personas around this assumption, but we quickly learned that our customers were spread out across the UK in more remote and isolated areas, and who were typically in the 35–44-year-old age bracket and older.

How to create a customer persona

Creating personas is a fun exercise, and when we move to other sections of this book around marketing and advertising you will see that personas are a useful tool for helping you grow your business. When creating personas you need to collate any existing information about your customers, and crucially consider how you can collect information about your customers going forward.

There are a number of great persona templates online. You'll find what we think are the best ones available in The Making a Living Programme. These templates will prompt you to fill in information into different sections. This can be daunting if you're feeling low on customer insight, but you might be surprised at how much you are already able to guess.

Here are some ideas to help you get started with collecting this information:

- *Write a paragraph about who you* think *your customers are,* based on what you've gleaned so far. Describe them as far as possible – male/female, age, where do they live, and so on.

- *Look at your main competitors,* especially the biggest ones. You can probably get an indication of who they think their target market is based on their advertising imagery, language and more. Remember that these large players will be working off large swathes of sales data, so if your biggest competitor looks to be targeting a specific demographic, then you might assume that they know they have a market here.

- *Carry out research.* Some of the bigger crafts organizations have useful resources to help you to get a national picture of audiences for crafts, and can even help you define audiences for specific crafts. This useful tool from the Crafts Council in the UK allows you to search data collected by its recent survey of the market for craft:

  https://www.craftscouncil.org.uk/about/research-and-policy/market-for-craft/market-for-craft-data-tool

- *Use Google Analytics.* If you have set up Analytics on your website already, you can start seeing who is visiting your site, giving you information on age, gender, interest, language, location, what device they are using and more. Google offers lots of free training on how to set up and use Analytics through its Google Digital Garage initiative: https://learndigital.withgoogle.com/digitalgarage/courses

- *Carry out surveys.* Surveys are a really useful way for small businesses to learn quickly about their customers. You can create surveys using free tools such as Typeform, or as mentioned earlier use Instagram Stories and its survey badges to ask simple questions. Don't be put off by small datasets. When you're starting out, just getting any information about your customers will be really useful and you'll be surprised at just how quickly themes will start to emerge about the make-up of your customers.

- *Conduct customer interviews (and conversations).* You can also consider doing a range of interviews with your customers and try to find out more about them. If this feels too formal, then simply having a longer chat with a customer at a market might help you with some interesting information to feed into your persona research.

You can also have more than one persona, so don't worry if you feel that you have a number of customer types to market to – plot them out separately.

A persona template may prompt you to complete the following fields:

- name [give your persona an actual name – e.g. Deborah]
- age
- gender
- education
- location
- employment
- visual [search for a photograph or illustration that you feel best illustrates your persona].

How are your values aligned with those of your customers?

If you put yourself into the mindset of your customers, you'll be better equipped to understand how to market your products or services to them. This might sound like corporate marketing language that is irrelevant to an independent craft business, but there are likely to be shared values that your customers have that correspond to your handmade products.

For example, it might be that you discover that your customers like to buy from independent sellers or to buy locally, are particularly interested in makers who are using recycled materials, or are keen to learn a new making skill in order to relax. How do your values as a maker or craftsperson align with theirs, and are you clearly communicating this enough to them?

Persona behaviours and habits

Figure 3.1 shows a sample persona developed for Yodomo after several users were interviewed directly and 100 users were surveyed using the surveying tool Typeform.

Behaviour and habits:
- Spending his off-screen time making useful, practical projects
- Recreational activities on weekends and evenings
- He likes to teach his friends what he's learned
- Learns by trial and error

Pain points:
- Finds cleaning up annoying
- Frustrated to find the course bought is superficial and unclear

Needs and goals:
- Knows what he wants to learn next
- Looking to do something interesting outside work
- A course with a skilled instructor where he can ask questions and interact with peers

"I figure out what I need to learn then I look for it online"

"I love zoom courses because I can ask questions and interact with the group"

Ben
Occasional Crafter
34 / London / Project Manager

Figure 3.1 A sample persona developed by Yodomo

Using these personas you can start to group together known behaviours and habits, pain points, needs, goals and more. Trying to get to the heart of what motivates your customers to buy from you or come to your live workshop will help you in your brand development and marketing strategy as you grow your business.

Other fields to consider at this point might include:

- goals / interests / motivation
- pain points / frustrations
- customers' relationship with technology or social media.

You'll see from the range of templates available that a persona can be as basic or in-depth as you want. As a small business starting out, we would recommend starting with a basic template and building on that as you start to get more customer data or meet with more customers, and simply edit and iterate your personas as your business grows until you feel you have settled on a balanced understanding of who your customers are.

Daily activities of your personas

Once you have jotted down your persona's vital statistics, the next step is to map out what their day looks like. This will help you to consider where best to meet your customers and using what medium. For example, do they commute to work, do they listen to a podcast in the morning, do they buy their lunch from a food market at lunchtime, do they drink craft beer in the evening? And so on.

This is also something that can be easily visualized with a simple timeline. Map out, even if just with pen and paper at first, what a customer's day looks like, taking special notice of where they go, what they read or listen to, who they interact with and so on. The point of this exercise is to consider what their daily rituals are and how your product of service might interact with that.

Niche markets

While you might think that this kind of exercise is for the sole use of larger brands, you'll quickly see that useful themes will start to emerge and help you frame your business strategy. As an example, perhaps one of your personas is really into health and wellbeing, and you decided that your handmade aromatherapy candles could find a market working in partnership with a local chain of yoga studios rather than trying to sell them through regular craft shops. This could also have an impact on your marketing strategy, and you might decide, as a result of considering your persona's daily habits, to partner with a micro-influencer on Instagram who works as a wellbeing consultant.

Don't be afraid if you feel that you seem to be targeting a very niche market as this could really play into your favour as you grow your business. As you will learn, it is actually much easier to target a specific niche within a larger market, rather than trying to reach everyone.

Even for small businesses there is real value in the exercise of getting to know your customers and their values, understanding their personal goals and pain points and using this information to better market your products and services to them. In later chapters we will revisit our personas and use them in marketing and advertising strategies.

Exercise

1. Create at least two personas for your handmade goods or crafts workshops.
2. Sketch out who they are, what their daily routines are like and give your personas names.
3. Consider the other areas of interest of your persona – where do they shop, what do they listen to, what brands might they align themselves with?

You can access persona and 'day in the life' templates from The Making a Living Programme.

4

Selling Online

For craftspeople and makers there are a number of revenue streams that can possibly be generated from one small business. These might include:

- selling handmade products directly online;
- selling handmade products via a third party (trade);
- selling handmade products in-person (crafts fairs, markets, gallery, retail);
- selling kits of materials and a guide to make something similar in your range;
- selling an online course of the skills and techniques that you have learned to others;
- selling an in-person workshop teaching your skills and techniques.

In this chapter we are going to look at the ways you can hone your offer and start selling online.

Selling handmade products

You don't need to have a wide range of products to launch a business; indeed, having a single product or single design focus can actually be beneficial not just at the beginning but throughout a business's life.

If you are already producing a range of products, you are likely to know what your best-selling items are, so it may be best to consider growing out a range from your best-selling items rather than constantly creating new products.

For example, if you're a macramé artist and you know that your macramé plant hanger is always the best-selling item at every crafts fair, then consider if you can expand that range of products with different colour options and so on rather than coming up with a whole new product. At the beginning it's advisable to become known for one hero product and to get that right, and to expand your product range only as your business grows.

Getting started does not have to be an expensive operation, and there are also plenty of ways to test out your products early on with audiences before investing in large-scale production or marketing.

Platforms such as Shopify and Squarespace have made it easier than ever to start selling online, and this can be a great option for growing a business without any physical overheads.

There are several ways that you can sell your products online, and we will look at each of these in detail. They include:

1. on your own e-commerce website;
2. through a marketplace seller such as Etsy, Not On The High Street or Yodomo;
3. on a third-party website (e.g. gallery or online retailer).

At the beginning of your e-commerce journey you should consider the simplest starting point for you. This may vary depending on your digital skills.

1 YOUR OWN E-COMMERCE SITE

Having your own site gives your business a destination for you, your products and your brand. There are pros and cons to setting up your own online store.

Pros

- You have full control over how and where your products are positioned.
- You can set your products in your own branding.
- You are not competing with other products from different sellers.
- You don't have to pay a commission.

Cons

- You will need to set up your own website, and if you're not particularly digitally savvy this might take up a lot of your time to get it right.
- There will be transaction fees when using PayPal and Stripe (there's more on these payment mechanisms below).
- You will have to work hard to drive traffic to your website.

Deciding on your e-commerce platform

One of the reasons it's a great time to start selling your products online is that e-commerce software is now readily available, easy-to-use and affordable. If you have an existing website, you might now have e-commerce available as part of your software package. You will want to establish, if you don't know already, which content management system (CMS) you are running from.

WordPress is a popular content management system because it is low-cost and has a basic version which you can customize with 'plug-ins' that allow you to add new features to your website. It is flexible for all kinds of content and easy to customize. Lots of developers know how to use WordPress, so if you get stuck you will be able to find someone with experience quite quickly. In addition, because so many people use WordPress you'll find that other software that you might need to use, such as Mailchimp or Facebook, will integrate easily with WordPress.

Once you've chosen a theme in WordPress, you can easily drag and drop content onto your site. While WordPress is easily customizable, anyone not used to using a content management system might find the interface a bit overwhelming, and if you're not familiar with using plug-ins, then installing these might be off-putting.

If you are already using WordPress for your website, you can add e-commerce functionality using a plug-in called **WooCommerce**. If you've run your site on WordPress for a long time, you won't have to move all your existing content to a new system, but you will need to ensure that the user experience flows logically and that your shopping cart and checkout pages are all set up properly.

You may find, however, that you will have to rewrite many sections of your site to adjust it to an online store. Consider that by the time you've reconfigured an existing site to e-commerce you may have spent the same amount of time setting up on a platform built specifically for e-commerce.

Platforms built specifically for e-commerce

Selling your products on a platform built for e-commerce can save you a lot of time and effort because all of the thinking has been done for you. There are now numerous communities built around these platforms, so you can work through any issues quickly as there is invariably always someone who has had exactly the same experience as you. Two of the leading e-commerce platforms are Shopify and Squarespace.

Shopify was built for e-commerce and makes it extremely easy to start selling online. It offers thousands of different themes for you to choose from, so you can get started with a style that suits your brand straight away. Sections are intuitive and prompt you to ensure that you've entered the right information in the right places.

Shopify will prompt you to create product pages, product collections, news pages and more. It will also lead you to connect your store to your Instagram account, Facebook account, Pinterest board and more – so if you have social media platforms, these can easily be transferred into 'shoppable' places where you can meet your customers.

An easy-to-use dashboard will enable you to compare your sales month on month, year on year, and so forth, making it easy for you to track your sales progress, and also gives you interesting insights into your best customers and most popular products.

Before you start adding products to your Shopify account you might want to create a taxonomy for your products and collections so that you have a clear system for how products are grouped and listed.

Shopify is now widely used so it makes it easy to find support when you need it, and there are many verified Shopify Experts who can help you build your online shop. They offer good customer service, and you can raise 'tickets' with them if you have specific questions.

Squarespace is loved by creative entrepreneurs because its themes have been carefully designed with creative businesses in mind. You can have a browse of its range of designed themes, and it's likely that you'll see one that feels just right for your business.

One consideration with Squarespace's super-slick themes is that they are always shown off with amazing product photography, so you might want to consider whether your own photography is up to scratch and, if not, what impact that would have on the overall look and feel of that theme. We will look later on in this chapter at how you can also create great product photography yourself.

Other options for your online shop might include Wix, Weebly and more. It can be overwhelming to decide which platform to choose, but do your research and speak to others who are running online businesses to ensure that you find the right platform for you.

Choosing a platform

Our key recommendations when choosing a platform to sell products are the following:

- Ensure that you can navigate the platform that you decide on – if you need to ask someone each time you need to change something, then this will cost you time and money. There are many free or low-cost tutorials online for each platform, so watch these to get a sense of what each platform's 'back-end' or dashboard looks like.

- Avoid platforms that are too niche as you may find it harder to find a developer to work on it. The advantage of using the most widely used platforms is that there will be many developers who know it well and online community support to help you.

Create a launch checklist

Before you sell anything online you need to ensure that you have covered the essentials before going live. Some of these actions might be essential for launch, and some might be 'nice to have' – don't let the 'nice to have' actions hold you back.

Exercise

Before you launch your online store, use this checklist to ensure that you have everything covered!

1. Do your products need specific health and safety guidelines? (E.g. are there special requirements if you are selling to children?)
2. Are products sold as described? With handmade goods sometimes sizes, finish and so on can vary. Have you made this clear in your description? Are there considerations for customers about how they should care for this product?
3. Have you been clear to customers about shipping costs and services, and any tax implications if selling abroad?
4. Do your photographs reflect the handmade goods, and if you have set items in a lifestyle shot have you been clear which items are part of that product sale?
5. Have you checked that your billing information is all correct within the system? (You may at this juncture consider creating a business account – see Chapter 8: Managing Your Accounts and Tax).
6. Have you linked your social channels to your online store?
7. Have you run through a dummy run sale to ensure that everything is working properly?
8. Has your pricing considered your own costs, the platform fees, shipping and taxes?

2 ONLINE MARKETPLACES

Figure 4.1 How marketplaces work

An easy option for selling your products is to sell through an online marketplace. The term 'marketplace' is exactly what it sounds like – you are still responsible for keeping your 'market stall' or online shop up to date and dealing directly with postage and customer queries.

One of the biggest online marketplaces for handmade goods is Etsy, which is now a global marketplace for crafts and maker businesses. Not On The High Street is also another major UK player, hosting around 5000 sellers.

The advantages of selling through these major marketplaces are that you can set up your online shop relatively quickly, with few set-up costs. Any major technology issues are the problem of the marketplace, and there are countless communities and customer support options for any questions that you might have about selling your products.

These marketplaces have a lot of online traffic while you might be struggling to get people to your own online store. The disadvantages of the bigger players is that you may have discoverability issues: there may be many similar products, and as the platforms get bigger the range of products becomes diluted. Some makers also raise concerns about their product ideas being copied and then sold at competitive prices, so if you have a unique product you should look at ways to protect your designs. In Chapter 12: Legal Requirements and Intellectual Property, we will look at the ways you can trademark your business and protect your ideas.

Smaller, curated marketplaces can offer an online marketplace for your products and, while not able to compete with the bigger players in terms of customer numbers, might give a better chance of visibility and promotion along with other perks that come with working with smaller teams. You can also look at specialists or local online marketplaces to meet customers with your products.

You may find that there is a bit of trial and error as you hone online outlets for your works. You might want to trial certain products as 'exclusive' to some platforms to be able to meet the needs of certain customers at the right marketplace, with the right product and price point.

3 THIRD-PARTY WEBSITES

There are other partners you can work with to sell your products. For example, there might be a gallery that would like to represent you online, or a retailer that would like to buy some stock to sell through its own e-commerce store.

The advantages for working with other third-party retailers is that you can just take a step back and they will look after product photography, uploading, sales and fulfilment. The disadvantages of this are that you may have to pay a significant commission for the work that they put in – for some galleries this might be up to 50 per cent and for some retailers 40 per cent.

Product pages

Once you've decided on the options of where to sell your products online, you need to master what makes a compelling product page. The product page is the landing page for your product, and if you are driving traffic from social media or advertising, then this is normally set as the first page that your customers will arrive at.

The best product pages combine engaging copy with great imagery that drives a customer to buy. It is also important that the customer is absolutely clear what they are buying. If you have images of multiple products, ensure that the customer understands that the price is just for one product. If you style a product with any additional items, ensure that you articulate what exactly is for sale in the price.

View your product pages with the following considerations:

- *product photography* that is labelled for SEO (search engine optimization);
- *product description copy* that contains keywords to help customers find your products and dimensions where necessary;
- *clear pricing* including prices for variants (e.g. different colours) and shipping costs;
- *potential frictions for the buyer* – is there anything on this product page that they might find confusing?

Product photography

The old adage 'a picture is worth a thousand words' has never been truer, and right now is the time to really get to grips with how to consistently get good photography for your products and your business.

You may want to develop a house style that reflects your brand style or ethos. Studio Ranj is a ceramicist whose decoration makes bold use of colour, so Ranj's house photography style employs a plain grey background that gives a clean contemporary feel while allowing the colours to become even more eye-catching (Figure 4.2).

The advantage of a house style is that your customers become accustomed to your brand look, and there are also advantages when you start using these images on social media, as the algorithms are sophisticated enough to recognize where a brand is being consistent in its imagery and will reward you accordingly by serving your content to more people.

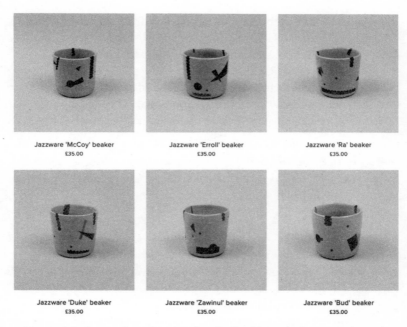

Jazzware 'McCoy' beaker
£35.00

Jazzware 'Erroll' beaker
£35.00

Jazzware 'Ra' beaker
£35.00

Jazzware 'Duke' beaker
£35.00

Jazzware 'Zawinul' beaker
£35.00

Jazzware 'Bud' beaker
£35.00

Figure 4.2 Screenshot showing Studio Ranj house photography style

While it's tempting to experiment with the hundreds of filters now available, allowing the customer to really see the product is of primary importance. On a product page we would always recommend having one clear, plain-backdropped shot of just the object itself. This is not to say that you can't also add images that have a more 'lifestyle' setting. For example, you might want to add images on the product page of somebody holding it or showing it styled on a mantelpiece.

When devising your house style, create a set of rules to adhere to. Below is an example of Yodomo's house style for photography.

Images should:

- be contemporary, bright and colourful without looking overworked;
- be in colour only;
- avoid desaturation, oversaturation, increased contrast, vignetting or HDR;
- avoid extremely shallow depth of field and wide-angle lenses;
- use natural light where possible or minimal lighting.

Creating a simple set of rules will allow you to create a house style that is just right for your brand. For example, a jeweller who is influenced by the sea might always choose to have at least one product shot on the product page that is on a rock with the sea in the background.

PHOTOGRAPHY TIPS

A light box can help even the most amateur photographers to get a good product shot. You can either create your own light box using cardboard or use one of a number of products on the market that make photographing finished products really simple.

You will also need to consider capturing the following images for your online shop:

- *a portrait of yourself* – a head-and-shoulders shot and a portrait of you, ideally working in your studio;
- *a flat lay of any materials needed to complete the project*, and a separate image with the materials supplied if you are selling a kit with your course (remember to be clear on what is provided in a kit, and what a customer is expected to have at home);

- *step-by-step photographs on the process of making* (if you've chosen to create a combined 'photographic steps and instructions' course, or what we call a 'hybrid' course – we explain more about these in Chapter 5: Selling in Physical Spaces);
- *your finished product* – a selection of standalone images, with the maker space in the background/foreground, or in a setting that is fitting for your products – for example with plants, on a beach.

To edit and resize photos you can use Photoshop if you have it. Canva is an easy-to-use and free alternative. There is a guide to using Canva in The Making a Living Programme.

FLAT LAY PHOTOGRAPHY

The flat lay photograph is now a standard for social media platforms such as Instagram and is ideal for showing multiple products at the same time or to demonstrate exactly what a customer will receive. To get a good flat lay image, ensure that your products are on a flat, ideally single-colour surface. If there are different colour choices for your product, take a photo of each one individually.

Ranjit Dhaliwal

Ranjit Dhaliwal was a picture editor at the UK newspaper *The Guardian* for 16 years before becoming a ceramicist. Here he gives his top tips for photographing products:

- Consider lighting and ensure that nothing in the room is causing a shadow onto your flat lay. We often do a flat lay on the floor and photograph overhead.

- Tuck your elbows into your waist as you're photographing to steady your shot and keep images sharp. Or try using a table, floor or something solid to steady yourself. Gorilla pods or similar small tripods are relatively inexpensive and can vastly reduce camera shake.
- Choose a consistent position and angle from where to take your pictures if you are doing multiple product shots, especially if they're going to sit next to each other on your site or social media grid. Professional photographers usually 'mark up' their spot with a cross of tape to remind them where to stand. A tripod can also help with this.
- Use natural light or a studio lighting kit rather than regular domestic lighting or on-camera flash.
- Using natural light is harder to control, and the weather or time of day can restrict when you can shoot, but there are a few methods that can help. Choose the brightest spot possible (near to a large south-facing window, beneath a skylight). Avoid harsh direct sunlight as this creates very hard shadows and reflections on shiny objects. You can diffuse hard light by draping a thin piece of white cloth like muslin or a net curtain over the window. Create your own reflector to help brighten your shots – white cardboard or aluminium foil wrapped around a stiff piece of cardboard box works well. Stand this upright, out of shot on the opposite side of your light source, to bounce the light back onto your subject.
- There are some decent, reasonably priced studio lighting kits available online. Choose one that comes with a softbox. A simple lighting set-up is two lights on opposite sides of the subject, pointed down at it at a 45-degree angle.
- There is no need to 'overinvest' in a really expensive DSLR camera just for product shots. All major manufacturers make affordable, easy-to-use compact cameras that are perfectly suitable. They are well worth investing in and will pay for themselves.

DOCUMENTING THE MAKING PROCESS

Customers love to see images of the making process, so try to capture as much good imagery of close-ups of skills and techniques, and where necessary include your hands making. You can ask someone to take photographs of you, or do this yourself using the auto settings on your camera or phone. On most camera phones and cameras you can set the timer to take your photograph in three or ten seconds' time, so you can set up the shot yourself.

There are also a number of inexpensive pieces of kit that can help you with these processes, including:

- a softbox lighting kit to help you get lighting right;
- a good digital camera (or upgrade your phone!);
- a background stand and Colorama backdrops (or create your own using fabrics);
- a selection of A1 mount boards for flat lay photography;
- a stand that enables you to position your phone at the right angle to capture a shot;
- an overhead arm or overhead table bracket.

If you want to find out more about developing a home studio photography kit, there is an up-to date list of recommended products in the Making a Living Programme, with personal recommendations from craftspeople and makers who have tried and tested different products.

As you start to regularly build product pages, you'll quickly realize that there are varying image sizes for each platform, so, for example, Shopify might have a different size specification to a marketplace. A top tip is to create templates for all the photography sizes that you use regularly, as this makes resizing images a much quicker process.

Other common troubleshooting issues with photography include:

- *pixelation* – if your image is looking blurred, then you may have downloaded the image from a site that has already reduced its size. Where possible, have a folder with your original photography in high resolution and work from those;

- *stretched images* – if you resize your images by dragging one side only, you will be stretching the image into a warped version of the original. Always resize proportionally by dragging from the corner.

PORTRAIT PHOTOGRAPHY

Many makers and craftspeople feel uncomfortable getting in front of the camera, but remember that many customers love to see the makers behind the products, as well as their studios and workspaces. If you have the budget for it, investing in some good portrait photography can help tell the story of your new business. Otherwise ask a friend or colleague to capture some imagery of you in action. Another option is to buy a remote control clicker for your mobile phone, which allows you to set up a shot and simply keep clicking the remote control clicker until you're satisfied with the shot, or simply use the timer setting of your phone.

Understanding SEO

Search engine optimization (SEO) is important for any business selling online and can have an impact on how your customers can find you. With website traffic being directed from various search engines (Google, Ecosia, Bing, etc.), understanding how to ensure that your products can be found by customers is an important skill to learn.

There are a few things to consider in making your online content more SEO-friendly.

Start by identifying some keywords that are associated with your products or workshops. Put yourself in the shoes of someone searching for a local workshop where they can learn to sew. If you wanted to learn how to use a sewing machine, you might type in something like 'How do I use a sewing machine?', 'sewing machine tutorial' or 'sewing machine for beginners'. In all three cases, the term 'sewing machine' was used. These are some of your keywords.

Notice that the action associated with each of the above searches is to learn something. In this case, you can use 'learn' as a keyword. Don't worry about using the exact phrasing. Search engines are sophisticated enough to understand the nuances of these searches.

Now that you have your keywords ('sewing machine' and 'learn'), you can start thinking about the components necessary to have an SEO-friendly page.

There are several factors that play into search engine ranking, but to begin with, you should focus on the following three:

1. *Title* Your title is important in that it's the first thing people will see in order to find out information about your product or service. Be descriptive as it is also one of the most important things that search engines pick up.

2. *Headlines* It's a good idea to think about what you want to convey about your product of service. Come up with a sentence or two that expresses this, and use these sentences as a heading using an 'H2' or 'Heading 2' tag. This will help search engines further rank your page among relevant searches.

3. *Description* Here is where you can include other keywords associated with your products or services. Think about what other keywords people might search when looking for a product or service like yours, and use them generously in the description.

SEO and images

SEO is not just for words. Search engines will also look for keywords that appear in alt text (alternative text – a short written description of an online image) as you load up images, and also look at how images have been labelled. Avoid uploading images as a series of nondescript numbers, but label each image clearly making use of your keyword research.

Getting paid: Stripe, PayPal, SumUp and more

There are lots of ways to get paid online, and by using established payment methods such as Stripe, PayPal or more, you can be assured that payment transactions will be secure. Most payment methods are straightforward to set up, and there is a wealth of support online to take you through the processes for each one.

When you set up your e-commerce shop or marketplace you will be prompted to enable a range of payment methods. If you want your customers to use their credit card, you can either use the payment method provider (e.g. Shopify Payments) or a third-party provider such as Stripe. Customers might also pay using PayPal or Apple Pay. When setting up your payment methods consider where you live and the behaviour of your customers. If you're shipping overseas, Shopify has a handy list of payment gateways that are available in each country: https://www.shopify.com/payment-gateways. This is a good way to research payment gateways that might be more common in other countries.

When setting up your payment methods check what fees are applied and when. You might be paying a fee to Shopify as the point-of-sale platform and then an additional fee to PayPal as the payment method. Where possible, chart this detail as all these micro-payments will be important to declare in your accounting and help you see where costs are being incurred.

Launching your store

Getting to the point where you are ready to launch your store is an important and exciting step – so congratulations if you've made it this far! While there is no physical cutting of a ribbon, consider some virtual ways to celebrate your online launch.

Before you launch, ensure that you have tested the customer experience as much as possible. Ask a friend or colleague to go through the entire process of getting to your product page, selecting a product, selecting a variant where applicable and buying the product. Ask for feedback on their experience, including checking any email communications they receive after purchase.

Most e-commerce platforms have a default set of messages for post-purchase, but you may be able to adjust this copy to make this part of the process as meaningful as possible. Consider where in the journey you can ask customers to sign up to your newsletter if you have one set up.

Once your online store is open you will need to:

• ensure that communications are coming directly to you so that you don't miss customer messages;

- keep your inventory up to date – most e-commerce stores will automatically change inventory in relation to sales, but if you're also selling directly at markets, then you may need to adjust this accordingly.

Getting your first order

Getting your first order can be at once exciting and terrifying. With most systems you will receive an email notification that you have made a sale and a second notification once the order has been paid for. In the order email you will be able to see:

- which product has been purchased and order number
- delivery address
- additional notes if there is a field for these, so you will need to look out for any personal messages that have come with the order such as a birthday note.

As an important note with online payments, you should always fulfil the items when payment is confirmed. One of the advantages of working with established e-commerce sites, such as Shopify, is that they will alert you quite quickly if there are any issues with the payment.

Once you have dispatched your item, it's important to mark your product as 'fulfilled' as this will normally trigger either a note to your customer that the product is on its way; on marketplace models it might be set up that you're paid only once the item is marked as delivered.

When you pack up your product, remember to ensure that you have:

- printed off a packing slip or included a receipt of purchase;
- included any special messages if the item is for gifting;
- provided adequate packaging, especially for fragile items;
- included marketing materials such as postcards.

Many customers today will expect packaging materials to be sustainable choices so consider your packaging materials carefully and communicate to your customer if packaging is compostable, recyclable and so on.

This overview of selling products online will help you to envisage the process from beginning to end, but there is more detail to come that will help you sell your products online.

Exercise

Build your first product page and work through this checklist:

1. Make sure that your product description is clear and accurate. Be sure to include information that customers might find useful before purchasing such as dimensions, materials and shipping details.
2. Create a range of images that positively represent your product range and a good set of portrait or studio images.
3. Consider SEO when writing copy and labelling your images.
4. Put yourself in the position of the customer and think about what questions you might still be asking when seeing the product page.
5. Have you set up payment options and are these clear to the customer?
6. Have you made it clear your policy on refunds and returns? (There's more information on refunds in Chapter 9: Customer Relations).

5

Selling in Physical Spaces

One of the biggest challenges that new businesses face in selling directly to customers is the cost of setting up a retail space. Luckily, for crafts and making businesses, there are lots of options to meet customers without having to commit initially to a decision to take on a retail space.

Physical spaces for selling to customers might include:

- crafts markets – regular markets where you can sell handmade products directly to customers;
- crafts fairs – traditionally, trade fairs where producers of handmade crafts can sell to trade retailers in bulk, but now often used in the same sense as the crafts market – that is to say, selling directly to customers;
- pop-up shops;
- galleries and open studios.

If you're starting out for the first time, simply getting out there and meeting your customers is a great way to get initial feedback on your products and to find out more about what potential customers are looking for. Don't procrastinate and agonize too much about going out with a perfectly honed brand or product range. Instead, see these events as an opportunity to hone your offering and really learn from what you see and hear.

Crafts markets and fairs

One of the biggest advantages of crafts or maker businesses is the craft markets or fairs that allow you to interact directly with customers. When choosing which market or fair to take part in, consider the following:

- whether it's an indoor or outdoor setting;
- the impact that weather will have on the event and your stock;
- whether there are opportunities for branding;
- whether there are any restrictions on what you can sell or any important health and safety aspects to consider, especially if it's a family event.

Consider, too, the time of year as any events tied to a traditional gift-giving part of the year are likely to be busier.

As you will have learned in developing personas around your customers, getting out into the field and selling directly to your customers is an excellent way to really start to build up market research about your industry, your competitors and your audiences.

Consider footfall when doing your research. Visit a number of different markets and try to speak to as many stallholders as possible to get a view on how busy they normally are.

A good way to compare markets is to grid out a number of different ones to work out which one is best for you. For example, you could create a small grid of the things that are important to you and create a simple comparison table:

	Price	Cover	Competition	Footfall	Price range
Church Crafts Fair	£15 per stall	Yes	Variety of stalls – no direct competition	Low	Low

(*Continued*)

	Price	Cover	Competition	Footfall	Price range
Teddington Crafts Market	£30 per stall	Mixed	Variety of stalls – some direct competition	Good	Low/ mid-
National Trust Craft Fair	£50 per stall	Yes	Many different stalls – higher end	Excellent	Mid– high– end

When looking at this in detail, you have to consider your own products and price points. If your handmade products, for example, are quite high-end, you might be better off paying more for the stall at, say, the National Trust Craft Fair as you know they have a good footfall and that their customers are willing to pay a bit more. You might consider sharing a pitch with another maker, as this is a great way to bring your overheads down and has some practical benefits: you can set up your stand together, go to the bathroom and have some company for the day.

DESIGNING YOUR STALL

Once you have decided on which crafts market you want to attend, the next step is to consider how your stall will look.

Before you start, check with the organizers whether there is a stand specification. This will help you consider how much stock to bring, how to dress your stand and anticipate any other restrictions that may have a bearing on how your stand will look.

Your stand at a crafts market or fair is a great chance to use your new business branding to capture the attention of customers. The temptation with a small space is to fill it up as far as possible with your stock. Sometimes, however, less is more, so consider exactly what you need to have on display.

Not all customers will want to engage in conversation with you, so consider bespoke signage that explains who you are, what you do, and how much your products cost, and ideally have some printed material that they can take away even if your customers are a bit shy or pushed for time.

Let your stall reflect your brand

The whole experience of visiting your stall should reflect your brand values down to the last detail. If you're running a sustainable business and your products are using recycled materials, then you don't want your customers seeing large plastic boxes under your stall or giving them a plastic bag to take away their products.

Ensure that your stall:

- is uncluttered (store additional stock carefully under your stand) and nicely branded;
- has space for marketing materials for customers to take away (business cards, leaflets);
- has a clear pricing list and labels that reflect your company's brand values and aesthetic
- shows off your products, including variants such as colour choices;
- is clear about not wanting customers handling products if they're very fragile, while encouraging them to ask questions;
- is as accessible as possible for all customers.

Some company branding can go a long way in helping customers to remember you. Banners don't have to look like you're selling services at a corporate trade fair. You can even consider designing something on a chalkboard or a light box. Make sure that there is some space in your stall where you can place branding without cluttering it.

At Yodomo's very first live event we used the cheapest letters for papier-mâché projects we could find in lieu of a banner, but these turned out to be really effective as you could see them from a distance and made a great backdrop for photography.

Your packaging is also a crucial opportunity for you to add your branding. This doesn't have to be expensive. Many makers and crafts people opt for a simple paper bag with a branded stamp, a very economical but effective option.

Using the work that you have done in creating your personas, consider what kind of stall design would appeal to them. Most crafts fairs and markets will have traffic coming from all directions, so consider what catches the eye when potential customers arrive at your stall. You should also consider ways to build up height for your stall, giving you more space to show off products regardless of how tall your customers are.

Accessibility, visibility, and health and safety

Always get on the right side of the market or fair organizers and let them guide you. If the event is over the course of a few days and you can see that some areas are getting a lot more traffic than others, it's always worth politely asking if they can rejig the stall plan to give other sellers a chance in the high-traffic areas.

Event organizers should have considered accessibility for visitors, but as a stallholder it's also your responsibility to ensure that everyone feels welcome and that both your products and the space around your stall are accessible.

Markets and fairs are often family affairs, so try to anticipate how to keep children occupied if their parents are shopping. A well-positioned or quick access toy can help to keep a little one entertained for five minutes of crucial shopping time.

Consider how your stall will be lit, and whether you need to bring some standalone lighting to put your products in the best light. Some night market organizers will offer lighting as part of their stand fee, but you might want to complement these with additional lighting that will specifically highlight your products and add some atmosphere. If you are bringing additional electricity extensions, be sure that the event organizer is happy with your set-up.

Once you've established your stall set-up, do your own health and safety check. Most crafts and maker markets will send someone around before opening to ensure that everyone is set up properly, but it's good practice to consider your own and your customers' safety and ensure that you've done as much as possible to protect your own stock.

Before trying a stall for the first time or experimenting with a new set-up, do a trial run first at home. This will allow you to stress-test any structural set-ups, lighting and more but without feeling stressed on site. Take a photograph of your ideal set-up at home to give yourself a blueprint to work from when you arrive.

Create a checklist to run through on the day so that you don't forget anything. Consider practical things like scissors, string, pens, bottles of water and snacks.

You should also check whether makers and craftspeople are required to have their own public liability insurance in place which will cover you for the duration of the event. (See Chapter 12: Legal Requirements and Intellectual Property, for more on public and employer liability.)

Michelle Drew

Michelle Drew spent 15 years working in the design industry before taking her passion for all things design to create Established 25, a zero-waste homeware and fashion accessories boutique combining contemporary design with quality craftsmanship with a nod to her Afro-Caribbean heritage. Here, Michelle shares with us a few of her top tips for selling at fairs:

- Always bring your best self and energy – people buy into your enthusiasm about your product and your journey into selling.
- Have a postcard or something with a QR code for potential customers to remember you with. People are always in a rush, so a QR code to snap and go is perfect.
- Get to know your fellow stallholders; they have a wealth of information and experience; especially if it's your first time selling.

SELLING THE LIFESTYLE

As a maker or craftsperson, you're not just selling the item but the lifestyle around it. Every part of the transaction is an opportunity for you to show off your brand and values. For example, taking our example of a jewellery designer whose designs are inspired by the sea, consider how using natural materials as props, such as driftwood and stone, will reflect the designs of the products themselves.

If your products have a function, then ensure that you have made this clear on your stand. For example, in our example of the macramé plant hangers, you'd want to ensure you have the healthiest-looking plants hanging from one. If you have household items to sell such as bowls or vases, consider the flowers or fruits that will best set off your products.

You might also want to consider bringing work that is larger scale, as this can act as a catalyst for a conversation about private commissions.

SELL YOURSELF!

Most buyers love to meet the makers or craftspeople behind products, so don't be afraid to speak about the work or the techniques involved.

If you're working in shifts with a friend or colleague, make sure the marketing on your stall makes it clear that your products have been handmade, so that this is easily understood whether you are there or not.

Most crafts buyers are fascinated by the process of making, so if you're at the stall, have a small making project on the side where you can show off some skills and techniques. This is also a good way to engage with customers and explain to them the time involved to make a product or the skills involved.

Emily Birkett

Emily Birkett, the curation and content manager at HemingwayDesign who organizes popular markets and projects throughout London, gives us top tips from the point of view of an event curator.

1. *First impressions are everything.* We spend a lot of time deciding whether we feel something is suited and complementary to our other offerings – the way you describe your brand on an application, the curation of your social media platforms (it's not all about how large your following is), the stores you've managed to secure as stockists or the carefully thought-through design of your stall at a fair. How you look from a public-facing standpoint is key. Spend time developing your brand to ensure everything feels aligned because if you can catch our eye and grab our attention, we'll know it's the right fit.

2. *Quality over quantity.* At HemingwayDesign, we pride ourselves in producing highly curated events. Alongside the aesthetic and design, how a product feels and stands the test of time is just as important in our eyes. We'd much rather see a smaller product range that has been carefully manufactured or curated than a large offering that feels rushed, off-brand or poorly executed. Investment in good practices, timeless design and quality products will develop a loyal customer base and benefit from repeat participation in markets.

3. *Figure out your purpose and tell your story.* There was definitely a reason for starting your company – there's a story to be told there. When challenging the big brands, you have to give people a reason for wanting to buy from you, as a small seller, rather than doing a quick online order. What drives you? Why did you start? Are you not for profit? Where do you manufacture? Are your products ethically produced and sustainably sourced? Those things are important and what customers, now more than ever, look for, are one of the many reasons they choose to shop small.

4. *Go the extra mile.* If you convince us that you'll hold your own and stand out at our event with an amped-up stall, bring along your best products, show initiative and cross-promote with us on social media and show that you mean business (pardon the pun), then you're on your way to getting us to book you in. It makes it easy for us to book you in the next time because we know you'll deliver.

5. *A rejection isn't final, so don't be disheartened.* Not all brands are right for every market but, equally, may not be right at this current moment. We highly recommend coming along to the market, looking at the brands we've accepted, checking out their online platform, how they present their stall, the quality of their products and try to envision where your brand could fit. Our markets are always open to repeat applications. Develop your product, your brand, and don't be scared to reapply a year or so later.

PRICING AND GETTING PAID

Ensure that your prices are clear and that you're not charging more than your online prices. You'd be surprised how many customers will do a quick check on their phone. You might want to offer a special discount for that day, incentivizing customers to purchase onsite.

As we move towards a cashless society, most stallholders now use a portable card holder such as SumUp, which enables you to easily take payment via all major cards and contactless services such as Apple Pay.

Take the time to set up your products in the card holder so that you can easily request payment. This will also make it easier for you after the event to know what was sold, so it doubles up as a way of charting sales and inventory.

Some customers may also want to pay in cash, so it's always worth having a cash box with a float ready.

Top tip

Make sure that you have sufficient power for all of the devices you might need at the event. It is likely that your card reader, tablet and phone will lose power throughout the day. If you're not near a power point, bring a portable charger with you.

MARKETING IN THE LEAD-UP AND DURING THE EVENT

Once you've booked your place at a crafts fair you can begin marketing to existing and potential customers. Work with the organizers to tap into their marketing and social media channels. Many events like to promote the event with 'Meet the Maker' interviews, so make yourself available in the lead-up to the event.

Use the event as a way of speaking to online audiences, too, such as creating Stories on Instagram of you setting up your stall, or using quiet times during the event to capture some good photographs or videos of the event.

Crafts markets and fairs are an excellent place to capture emails from customers or potential customers for future email marketing campaigns. Have a tablet ready and encourage people to sign up to a newsletter or ask customers if you can email their receipt to them, giving them an opt-in/opt-out option for your newsletter at the same time.

GETTING THERE

Most crafts markets and fairs will have strict set-up and drop-off times and locations if you are bringing things onto the site in a vehicle. Create a simple timeline to ensure that you leave yourself lots of time to pack up your things and travel to the event. Enlisting the help of a family member or friend should make carrying heavier objects easier. Sometimes just having one other person to wait by the vehicle if you're unloading can be really helpful.

Pop-up shops

With the high-street landscape changing rapidly, the opportunity to take on a pop-up shop for a short period of time has never been greater. It's a fantastic way for makers and craftspeople to sell to the public, without having to take on the commitment and cost of a permanent shop.

As the pop-up market has grown, so too has the number of ways that you can find stores. You can either contact landlords of a property that looks like it is available and pitch to them a short-term lease or contact your local council to see whether it is running any schemes to encourage the temporary use of vacant properties. You can also approach shopping centres, which often run schemes to allow small businesses to pop up for a short time. There are now also a growing number of services to help you find vacant commercial properties such as Appear Here and Sook Spaces.

As with crafts markets, choosing the right location is crucial. Do your research and ensure that the property has adequate footfall and the right clientele.

Tabara N'Diaye

Tabara N'Diaye is the founder of La Basketry, a lifestyle brand which began by offering handwoven homeware and accessories made in collaboration with female artisans in her native Senegal. She has since gone on to release her debut book, *Baskets*, a stylish guide to basket-making, now available in six languages. Before running her own small business, Tabara worked as an event manager – running everything from trade shows and street food markets to charity events and festivals – so has a great understanding of what it's like to take part in an event from both sides.

Here are some of Tabara's top tips on making sure your pop-up event runs smoothly:

1. *Public liability insurance (PLI)* This is essential for any market or event you want to do, and you should make sure that this is something the organizers require. If they don't, I would be hesitant to sign up for an event that doesn't take the legal aspect seriously! (Refer to Chapter 12: Legal Requirements and intellectual Property, for more on PLI.)

2. *Comfortable shoes* This is a no-brainer – event days are long! From setting up in the early morning to breaking down your stall, you want to make sure that you have comfortable shoes for the day. Sandals are cute for a summer event, but are they really that comfortable after ten hours on your feet?

3. *A fanny pack/bum bag with some craft essentials* This might hold a pair of scissors, some tape, some string, a couple of pens, a spare phone charger, and any other stationery you may need for the day.

4. *Thank you cards with a discount code* You want to encourage people to shop with you again, so definitely get some flyers printed with a discount code that customers can redeem online on their next purchase.

5. *A new product/idea to gather feedback* As you will be in direct contact with potential customers, this is a great opportunity to test out a make or product you have been working on and get some initial feedback.

6. *Offer a free sample/demo a product* Free samples don't always work but are a good way to drive some footfall and start conversation. Demonstrations are always a win-win. Could you run a couple of small and free ten-minute workshops every other hour, so people have a better understanding of what you are selling?

Galleries and open studios

Exhibiting work in a gallery or sharing an exhibition with a group of like-minded makers and craftspeople is a great way to showcase your work and meet new customers. The advantage of working with a gallery is that they will do a lot of the heavy lifting for you. They will also have an existing clientele to share your work with.

Some makers have two very contrasting revenue streams – one that meets a high-end gallery audience and one that is more mainstream and commercial. This will often be determined by the way products are made. Where makers and craftspeople might create bespoke, handmade pieces for the top end of the market, they might also create accessible kits for simple projects that you can do at home.

Doing your research and finding the right gallery is your first step. You should consider the range of work they have exhibited in the past, look at their pricing and consider their likely customers. You will be able to glean quite a bit of information from the makers whom it already represents.

Most galleries will have clear instructions on their site about how to contact them and what their selection criteria is. When working with a gallery you will want to establish their terms and conditions, especially around exclusive representation and commission.

Depending on where you live you might have the opportunity to participate in a local open studios initiative and take advantage of exhibiting as part of your community, pooling audiences in this way across a large group of artists and makers.

For example, Crouch End Open Studios, a celebration of the vibrant art scene in London's Crouch End, offers the opportunity to meet and talk to local artists, browse and buy direct from them. Established in 2004, the event takes place annually and attracts thousands of visitors every year. The artists involved in Crouch End Open Studios work in a range of media, including ceramics, drawing, glass, mixed-media, painting, photography, print and sculpture. The event involves both established and emerging artists producing work to a high standard.

Julia Clarke

Julia Clarke, part of Crouch End Open Studios, is an artist who works with willow, cane, thread and ceramics. Julia works to make sculpture and craft accessible to all and believes it can really help people connect and be inspired. Her sculptural work has been exhibited at Kew Gardens, Alexandra Palace Art Trail, Cambridge Contemporary and commercial galleries throughout the UK. Here, she offers some insight into the journey of exhibiting with galleries and art spaces.

Having the confidence to approach galleries is the first hurdle. Once you've got a small collection of work that you love, photograph it as professionally as you can and send it directly to the gallery. Find galleries that you think your work will fit with. Once you're in, don't be scared to show them different types of work and ask for their advice.

Open studios are a really good way of seeing how people like your work. You can sell directly and take commissions. It's a good idea to get involved as these things won't happen without lots of extra work. I have found my local open studios so fulfilling and have made brilliant contacts and good friends.

I've had galleries approach me from my Instagram account and through open studios. Kew Gardens approached me because I could exhibit with them and run family workshops. Public art jobs often want you to be both a fine artist and workshop facilitator.

My last piece of advice is: don't compromise! Try to stick to what you want to make, because if you become too commercial then the work itself will suffer.

Exercise

You will have seen in this chapter that there are a few themes emerging when selling in physical spaces:

1. Consider what you can go out with as an initial range of products and how you will gather feedback from customers.
2. Create your own health and safety checklist for public events that you can tick off, whether it's a market, pop-up shop or other public event.
3. Create a compelling offer on a postcard that will encourage people you meet at public events to find out more about your work online.

6

Selling Your Skills

So far, we have focused on the myriad of ways that you can sell your finished products, whether that's selling handmade products online, at a craft market or through a gallery. For craftspeople and makers today, there are also a growing number of revenue streams emerging from the sharing of crafts and making skills and techniques. These might include:

- selling an online course that teaches the skills and techniques that you have learned to others;
- selling crafts or maker kits of materials along with a how-to guide;
- selling an in-person workshop teaching your skills and techniques.

In this chapter we'll look at each of these opportunities in turn.

Developing online courses

The market for online learning has been growing rapidly for the past few decades and is projected to grow even larger as consumers' attitudes to learning remotely are changing. Thankfully, the crafts and maker community has been an early adopter to learning online, with a huge community of crafters and makers sharing their skills online through videos on **YouTube**. YouTube offers great quick-fire tutorials for projects, and many people around the world are happy to share their skills for free.

There is also a growing market for *paid-for* online tutorials, where skilled instructors can load up their skills into a 'learning management system', or LMS, and protect that content behind a paywall.

In 2017 we interviewed several professional makers and crafters about their appetite for sharing their skills and knowledge online. Three themes emerged:

1. Makers and craftspeople do not always want to give away skills that they have learned and honed over a long period *for free.*

2. Makers and craftspeople do not always feel confident in the production skills needed to create quality digital content (video and photography) that matches the high quality of their handmade goods.

3. Some makers and craftspeople are worried about online communities associated with sharing content, and didn't want to receive negative comments about their content.

The big advantage for makers and craftspeople in developing a paid-for online course is that, once created, it can help to create an additional revenue stream to their practice, which can tick away even while they are delivering live workshops or making new handmade products to sell.

Emerging online course systems such as **Teachable** and **Thinkific** have allowed a greater number of makers and craftspeople to share their skills and knowledge online within easy-to-use learning management systems. These learning management systems allow learners to retain their courses in one place, remember where they got to in the course and follow a logical approach to learning.

For instructors, learning management systems offer the chance to easily monetize online courses, the opportunity to build audiences with people who are genuinely interested in their craft, the opportunity to generate income from their skills and techniques with learners from around the world, and more control over who sees content publicly and who can comment on content.

Many makers, craftspeople, designers and artists already have a tried-and-tested 'live' workshop format that they are used to hosting at public and private events. When approaching the development of an online version of such a workshop there are specific considerations to take into account.

PLANNING YOUR COURSE

Before you begin filming or photographing anything, it is always recommended to properly plan out your course. The first step in planning is to do your research. Make sure to look at existing courses in your field to understand the space that you will be competing in.

Top tips

- Research what your competitors and collaborators are doing in this space and see where you can add value or originality.
- Consider your target audience – that is, 'Beginner', 'Intermediate' and so on – what is already available for this audience?
- Consider whether the learner will need specific skills to complete the course.

RISK ASSESSMENT

Part of planning your course is assessing the risk of your activity. Ask yourself:

- Who is the course designed for? Is it suitable for all ages? Can children safely do the course? Will children need adult supervision? Make sure you clearly state the target audience.

- What tools and materials are required? Are they sharp/dangerous? Always advise learners on best practices when using and storing tools and materials.

- Safety equipment – do you need to wear specific or protective clothing? For example, does the activity require eye protection? Make sure you give clear and detailed safety instructions.

Workshop space – do the learners need to work in a specific space or set-up? For example, do they need to be outdoors or in a well-ventilated space? It's important to identify the set-up required to complete the course safely.

NAMING YOUR COURSE

Make sure that you remember to consider search engine optimization (SEO) when you are naming your course (see Chapter 4: Selling Online for more on SEO). Your title is important in that it's the first thing people will see to find out information about your course. It's also what search engines will pick up. Make use of your keywords to convey what your workshop is about, and use these keywords in your course title.

CREATING SECTIONS OF YOUR COURSE

You will need to consider how your course might be divided into sections and map out the different stages and steps of the learning process. Sections create a staged learning process, which is logical and easy to follow. These sections can be viewed sequentially or revisited in any order. However, make sure that each section is a fulsome learning experience and not just there for padding.

Learners of crafts are interested in the historical context of arts and crafts skills and techniques, so including information about the history of your craft (if applicable) is a recommended addition to the introduction of your online course.

In addition, learners are always inspired by the personal stories of their instructors, so we would always recommend a section that explains who you are, how you came to your craft, who inspires you and your journey to becoming an expert in your field.

Sections should:

- be well researched
- have a logical place in the course
- add specialist knowledge
- give the learner a unique course experience that is unlikely to be duplicated anywhere else on the internet
- bring added value.

Break down the content as far as possible. You might initially think that your online course is a simple three-section process, but the first thing to consider is whether there are 'hidden' sections that need to be added in. What are the skills and techniques that come naturally to you but might need explaining to someone coming to this activity for the first time?

You might be concerned that some course content is far too obvious to be explained – but this may not be necessarily the case for the learner. Do a rigorous analysis of the creative process and consider where additional sections would be beneficial.

For example, if you wanted to create a course on 'Smoke-firing a pot', you might initially suggest that this activity has three simple sections:

1. Building a smoker
2. Smoking pot
3. Polishing finished pot

However, with so few details, this will leave the learner with more questions than answers. Here's an alternative set of sections:

1. Meet the maker (an introduction to the instructor and their experience).
2. What you will learn.
3. What you will need.
4. Choosing your pot to be fired.
5. Fire pit equipment and safety.
6. Building the fire pit.
7. Choosing materials that will colour your pot.
8. Taking out your pot and washing it.
9. What next? (Tips for new projects, caring for your pots, etc.)

To help you plan your course, several free planning resources can be accessed at yodomo.co to guide you in mapping out these sections.

Once you've broken down your online course into sections, double-check the following:

- Are the sections clear and easy to follow?
- Are all learning aspects of the proposed course thoroughly considered and included if necessary?
- Is there adequate content to warrant the course and its price?
- Have you pinpointed opportunities where you can add extra sections to create a value-packed learning experience?

COURSE FORMAT

When planning your online course, you need to put yourself in the place of the learner and consider any questions that they might have. Some course content formats lend themselves better to learning than others, and putting yourself in the place of the learners will help you to decide which format will work best for your online course.

Online courses can be delivered in many different ways. Three of the most popular online course formats for crafts are:

1. video
2. step-by-step photography and text
3. hybrid (video, photography and text).

1 Video courses

One consideration at this stage of planning is how you feel about getting in front of the camera. Many makers and craftspeople are very confident with teaching face to face but find the sudden added pressure of being in front of a camera daunting. Any reluctance to get in front of the camera can be mitigated by focusing as much as possible on the hands.

If you're shooting a 'Meet the Maker' video, you may find it is easier to do at the end of your filming day, because it's at this stage that most makers and craftspeople start to feel a bit more comfortable in front of the camera.

2 Step-by-step photography and text courses

A simple online course can be created from just photography and text. The advantage of this format is that you need fewer skills to create these courses. The disadvantages are that there are only a limited number of things you can show through photography. You may find that video content is really necessary to show in detail a specific skill.

Figure 6.1 shows a step from the 'Make a willow star' course by artist Julia Clarke and is an example of how simply you can use photography and text to take a learner through steps.

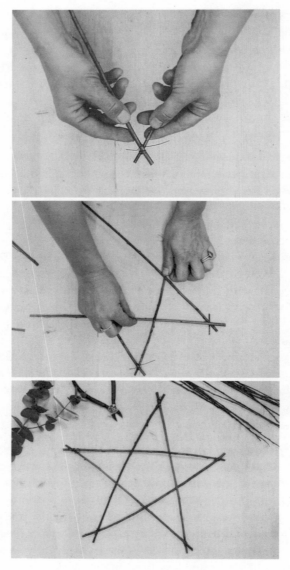

Figure 6.1 Step 4: Construct the star; Julia Clarke online course photographed by Kathrin McCrea for Yodomo Ltd

Text instructions: Weave the star shape under over, under over, then attach the points with wire to keep them secure. Lay the star shape out in front of you to make sure it is right.

3 Hybrid courses

As mentioned above, some stages of learning will always be better explained with video content. Shooting video content is often more complicated and can incur additional expenses, but some courses can lend themselves well to shooting in both photography and video. These 'hybrid' courses mean that you can use photography to shoot simpler steps (for example, a flat lay photograph of the materials and tools you will need) and save the video filming for more complex sections (for example, an action such as tying a knot which might be hard to see in a photograph).

In crafter By-Me Katie's 'Make a spiral knot macramé plant hanger' course, she uses a hybrid format. To illustrate some of the simpler steps, she uses photography and text. For close-up detail, however, of the knots, she uses video to demonstrate the spiral knot (see Figure 6.2).

Figure 6.2 Screengrab from By-Me Katie's 'Make a spiral knot macramé plant hanger' course for Yodomo Ltd

CREATING VIDEOS

You can also choose to film your entire course using video. The advantages of this are that you can lift an existing live workshop format almost verbatim into an online course without too much prior planning. It also helps explain specific techniques and tools that may require a video demonstration in order to explain fully. The disadvantages of video-only are that you will either need a good grasp of video content creation and some decent editing skills or have to find someone who has these skills. Below are the steps to consider before you get heavy into the tech.

Preparing a script

Once you have your course sections and have considered the content format of your course, you can begin to write your filming script. If you choose to create your course from photography and text only, this script writing exercise can be adapted to write the text for each section.

The easiest way to approach this is to carefully consider the learner's perspective and ask questions about each stage. Be inquisitive. Be robust. Your goal is to create a rigorous course that harnesses your expertise, specific experience and knowledge.

There are many free or low-cost storyboarding and scriptwriting tools now available including:

- *Plot* A free and fast storyboard creator.
- *Storyboarder* An open-source, free storyboarding tool that makes it easy to visualize a story.
- *Scrivener* A tailor-made tool for long writing projects, helping you to compose your text in any order, in sections as large or small as you like.
- *StudioBinder* Free, professional screenwriting software.

In our additional resources (see below) there is also a free planning guide to help you script your sections.

Use questions and other research to inform your filming script and/or your descriptions of each section. From our example of a Smoke Firing Ceramics course, the instructor put themselves in the place of the learner and ensured that the content answered these questions:

- When do you know it's ready?
- Can you take it out at different times and what's the effect?
- Do some smokings (e.g. raku) last longer than others?

- How do you retrieve the pot from the fire safely?
- What if the fire goes out?
- What if your pot breaks?
- What if it comes out black or with not much colour on it?
- Can you learn from the disappointment?
- Are there any special techniques at this point?
- Where is best to wash it? Do you do that immediately or wait?
- What do you wash it in?
- Could your pot break on contact with cold water?
- Do you leave it to try? For how long?
- What do you put on it now?
- If you wax it, what wax do you use?
- How do you apply it?
- When do you know it's finished? (Explain the finished item).

Top tips

- Try to give light and shade to each section by including instruction, a fact, extra information such as alternatives to try or pitfalls to avoid, and, if it's of value, a short anecdote or information with a historical, social or environmental reference. The aim is to create a fulsome, rounded experience for the learner.
- Remember that if you're describing something then the learner needs to be able to see it. Keep any pieces relevant to the action in front of the camera.
- Be descriptive, verbalize clearly what you can't communicate visually (e.g. the dough's texture).
- Be clear on what is going to be different when learners do this at home.
- Communicate clearly about leaps in time, if any (e.g. leave the dough in the fridge overnight).
- The filming script is not a script for you to learn by heart. It's there to help keep you on track, to use as a prompt, and to make sure you get to the relevant action at the right time.

Hosting a video guide or online course

If you're creating a video guide to accompany your kit, consider how the customer will access it. You can use platforms such as Vimeo, YouTube or Teachable to host your video, each of which has its pros and cons. **Vimeo** has password protection for videos, but only for premium (paid) memberships. **YouTube** doesn't offer password protection but instead provides unlisted videos. This means anyone with the link can access them, but they won't show up in their search. **Teachable** has a great format for courses, and you can host videos and images alike, but there is a fee to using it.

Alternative ways to give access to your video content includes a **DropBox** or **Google Drive** where only those invited to view would be able to access it, or you may be able to embed a video on your website and password-protect the page.

PRICING YOUR ONLINE COURSE

Pricing something that's immaterial is difficult to get your head around, but a good place to start is to consider the number of hours you put into learning your skills, putting the course together, and any overheads you might have, such as software and selling platforms. You may also want to develop a kit that will go along with the course. Continue reading below to find out how to develop and price a kit. There is also a comprehensive overview of how to price your course in Chapter 8: Managing Your Accounts and Tax.

Templates

Now that you have a clear understanding of online courses and how to plan your online course, you can move on to the next stage of creating your content. Access our downloadable PDFs from The Making a Living Programme to help you with the planning stages of your online course.

Developing a crafts or maker kit

While there are countless commercial crafts kits on the market, many learners prefer the authenticity of learning from an independent maker or craftsperson.

As a first step, it's important to undertake a bit of competitor research, as understanding the market your kit will be competing in will help you hone your offer.

Start by outlining what you want to teach – whether it's a creative skill or the steps of making a completed object, or else mastering a craft. Write this down, then think about how you'd want to learn this. For example, should your course be project-based? Do you want your students to leave your course with a completed object? Are there specialist tools or equipment you'd like your students to know how to use by the end?

Note down all the relevant information so that you can refer back to this when you're putting the kit together.

It's always a good idea to look at what potential competitors are offering and seeing where you can fill any gaps. Differentiating your product will give customers good reasons to buy from you. Search for kits and courses similar to what you'd like to create and make a note of anything that overlaps with what you have in mind. Then, list out what you like about each of them, as well as what you're not so fond of. This can be anything from the materials used to the packaging.

Exercise

Use these questions to help you to research your kit:

1. What do you want to teach?
2. What are other, similar makers doing?
3. Who is your target audience?
4. What information should you include in your accompanying guide?

INVESTMENT NEEDED TO DEVELOP YOUR KIT

The goal is to make a profit from your accompanying crafts kit, but it does require time and initial investment, however small, to produce a kit and course. It will help to budget out your resources and materials from the get-go so that you can keep track of your expenses and figure out pricing easily.

Consider what you can afford and be strict with yourself on this, and consider everything that will cost you money before spending anything on kit materials. Here are some things to consider for your budget:

- materials for your kit (are there savings for bulk buying?)
- packaging materials, including shipping box, tissue paper, labels, tape and so on
- printed materials
- software, such as Teachable, Canva or Adobe subscription
- a test kit that you'll need to use to create images for marketing purposes
- a test kit to give to someone else to receive honest feedback
- marketing, such as advertisement on social media.

HOW WILL KIT INSTRUCTIONS BE INCLUDED?

Your course might come with a printed guide, an online guide with photographs and text, an online video tutorial or full course, or a combination of these. See the section above on creating an online course if you decide that your crafts kit is best experienced with an accompanying video or online course.

Planning out steps for a printed guide

Start by writing down the rough steps you want to include from beginning to end. Once this is done, go back and see whether anything is missing. Try to imagine what it might be like going through the steps if you do not know anything about the craft.

Similarly to online text and photographic courses, you can include a section on troubleshooting, top tips or a glossary towards the end, as well as top tips throughout the steps.

Once you're comfortable with the steps you've provided, take a look through the steps and list out all the materials you mentioned. This will be what is listed under 'Tools and materials' for both your marketing copy and your guide. You'll also be deciding on what to include in your kit from this list, so keep it handy.

Editing

Now that the rough draft has been laid out, carefully read it through, and reorder or adjust as appropriate. A sample order might include:

- introduction, including what learners learn or make
- brief history
- tools and materials (remember to flag what learners will need at home – e.g. hammer, apron)
- numbered steps
- tips, troubleshooting, glossary
- author biography.

Once the order is set, try following the guide through each step with the materials at hand. You might discover that there are small in-between steps you forgot to mention, or else there may be discrepancies in materials you need to address. Be sure to take careful notes and add in anything you find when you follow your guide.

Run your written guide through a grammar and spellcheck tool such as **Grammarly** to make sure there are no typos. You might also want to have a friend or colleague read over your copy, to see whether everything makes sense for someone with no background in your craft.

When you're happy with the copy, you can adapt it into your printed guide. This can also be used for an online course, as explained above.

Regardless of whether you're planning on creating a printed guide, an online course or both, you'll need striking images. See Chapter 4: Selling Online to ensure that you have the best photography to accompany your instructions.

When you have all of your photographs and copy, it's time to add them into a template. The best way to do this is to create each page as you would in the natural order and number them accordingly.

Then, once numbered, reorder the pages into booklet order. Your printer may not require you to reorder them and will print them automatically, but for those who will want a booklet order, take a look at Figure 6.3.

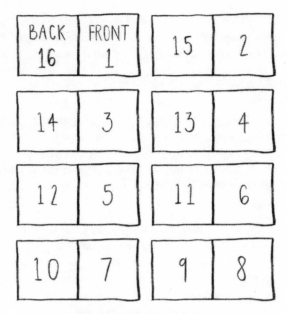

Figure 6.3 Booklet page order

There is a really handy page order calculator at www.boooks.org that tells you how to order your pages if you are printing double-sided with the intent of creating a booklet. Once printed, you'll need to bind the booklet either with a long-armed stapler or with a sewing needle and thread.

You might also want to consider getting your booklet printed at a print shop, where everything will be printed and bound professionally. This is great for saving time and can be cost-effective if you are ordering many, but can be expensive for each booklet if you're only ordering a few as a trial for your kit.

WHAT'S IN THE KIT?
When deciding what to put in your kit, refer to your list of tools and materials needed. What should you include in your kit? Things to consider here are what would be most cost-effective, as well as what people might already have in their home.

For example, for a painting kit, one might use an easel for their professional work, but including an easel in their kit would mean much higher shipping costs for an item that is not essential, especially for someone just starting who may not want to continue painting after the kit project has been completed. If you'd like a particular piece of equipment to be available to your customers, offering it as an add-on is a good idea.

Your project might also need everyday items such as masking tape, a tape measure, a pencil or a pen. In these cases, you can reduce cost by omitting them. Do make it clear to learners, however, what they are expected to have at home. When including a photograph of materials, if there is anything shown that is not included in the kit, be clear about this.

You probably know best where to source materials and tools needed for your kit, as they're likely the same ones you use for your practice. However, when you're buying materials for kits, they'll likely be in larger quantities but smaller units. Because of this, it might be worth exploring wholesale options or companies that offer discounts on bulk buys.

Wholesalers often require buyers to be registered as a business before purchasing from them, although there are exceptions. They often offer products at lower costs, but require a minimum spend. Search around on the internet or ask other makers for suggestions for wholesalers that might fulfil your needs, and get in touch with them to find out whether ordering from them is viable.

If purchasing from a wholesaler isn't possible, you might be able to contact your usual suppliers to see whether they're able to give you a bulk discount. Consider the amount of material needed for each kit, and whether this amount can be found pre-packaged or if you'll need to alter the amount. For example, if you're offering a macramé kit that needs 16 times one-metre cords, you may want to source a large amount of cord and cut them to the exact size.

POSTAGE AND PACKAGING

There are a few things that you'll want your packaging to do. It should:

- ensure your kit arrives at its destination fully intact;
- give your customers a great opening experience so that they'll be wowed when they open their package;
- be sustainable: can you minimize the use of plastic in your packaging?
- be cost-effective: how can you spend less on packaging while making sure nothing is damaged during shipping?

Once you're confident that your kit will be able to arrive safely at its destination thanks to carefully considered packaging, it's time to brand it. If it's within your budget, consider the customer's experience when opening your kit. It might be nice to have a branded sticker or a sticker that says, 'Thank you!' A postcard that features your brand or craft and a personal note is a great additional touch that adds another level of professionalism. A memorable first impression will lead to return customers and recommendations.

SHIPPING

If you're creating your kit for delivery, shipping is something you'll need to consider. There are many options for shipping, from dropping off your packages at the local post office to courier pick-up. Adding shipping into your final price and offering 'free shipping' can be a good way to simplify costs for customers but may make your kit price seem higher to customers. With free shipping, however, there is less of a chance that someone might abandon their cart once they see the extra shipping cost.

Be sure to manage customer expectations with shipping. If possible, outline how long it takes for a kit to dispatch (when it arrives at the post office) and how long delivery takes. You're not Amazon, and that's part of the reason why people will want to buy from you, but it also means you might not be able to fulfil next-day delivery. Communicate openly with your customers and they will more than likely be understanding.

TESTING

Once you have everything in place from kit to course, it's time for one more test (or many more, if you're feeling perfectionist). You can send it out to a friend or colleague or go through it yourself as if you yourself had received it in the mail. Ask for critical feedback from others on their experience of trying to finish the project using the kit and guide or course, then improve your kit accordingly.

PRICING

Pricing can be difficult to gauge because there are several factors that need to be taken into account. The first thing to do is to add up all the materials cost of your kit.

People tend to be understanding when you explain the cost of things. For example, while someone might be able to find cheaper macramé rope from a major retailer, its rope might not be 100 per cent cotton, might involve unfair wages for workers at the factory where it's manufactured, and may not come in a kit that has been thoughtfully designed by an experienced independent maker.

Customers pay for the materials, but they're also paying for your expertise, which has involved many years of perfecting your craft. This should be rewarded, so don't shy away from paying yourself a fair portion of the profits.

Any other costs should be on top of this final figure – for example, if a shop takes a commission or if you need to pay tax. You can download our simple crafts kits price calculator from yodomo.co to help you get to your final pricing structure.

It is always advisable to give yourself some room to price-promote from a higher price, rather than risk a lower starting price where there is no wiggle room for promotions or discounts because of a lean profit margin.

Developing in-person workshops

In-person workshops are increasingly popular at many different places, including galleries, retailers, hotels and museums, which are all looking to offer great experiences to customers through engaging workshops led by talented makers and craftspeople. It's always worth approaching some of these organizations directly, especially if you see them already running a programme of workshops. Another emerging revenue stream for makers and craftspeople is through developing a workshop that you can offer to companies to engage their employees. Engaging in crafts and making is known to boost productivity, mood and focus, so employers are always looking for great ideas to engage their employees.

WORKSHOPS FOR CORPORATE CLIENTS

Corporations will often have a budget for activities that are for the purposes of teambuilding, inspiring creativity, or just to keep their employees content and less stressed. Because of this, getting corporate clients for your workshops can be rewarding and lucrative.

More and more companies are incorporating creative workshops and events into their schedules as a way to motivate employees, support their wellbeing and boost creativity. Wooing corporate clients can be a daunting task, but these clients are valuable not only for the generally competitive rates they pay but also for the contacts it could provide and doors it might open.

In order to make your workshop a compelling offer for corporate clients, consider how it might add value to their organization or else support their bottom line. How will your workshop help increase productivity, and therefore profits? How might it nurture creative problem-solving skills? Will it bring more awareness to issues on sustainability or mental health?

Organizations will put aside money to be spent on these types of activities for a number of reasons related to supporting employees and improving productivity. Numerous studies have shown that creative activity and the act of making can boost mental wellbeing, improve morale and help with teambuilding. For organizations that want to promote sustainability, making also encourages careful consideration of materials used and slow living practices.

Determine the value your workshop has to offer and play into this when deciding how to market your workshop to corporate clients. Keep this in mind when you're planning out your workshop, ensuring that this value is built into the steps that participants will undertake or skills they will learn. If you can build in an alignment between the brand and the workshop, then this is a very compelling offer for a company.

Planning your workshop

Your workshop will likely begin with the skill you want to share, which you're an expert in. From this starting point, consider whether you want the workshop to end with a finished product or a learned skill. For example, if your workshop is on calligraphy, you could either have participants learn by practising on scrap paper, or else they can complete a greeting card that can be taken home and gifted.

Now that you have a concrete goal for the participants, start building your workshop towards this. Lay out the steps of what they'll need to know and do, and write down any extra information or tips that would be useful for them.

Consider the length of your workshop. A corporate client may not have an entire day to dedicate to a single event. Limit your workshop to an hour or two and give yourself enough buffer time in case something takes longer than expected.

It may be helpful to structure your workshop into sections. We recommend the following:

1. Introduce yourself.
2. Provide an overview of what they'll learn or make.
3. Detail the materials to be used.
4. Stress the safety considerations.
5. Give a history of the craft.
6. Demonstrate the technique.
7. Go through each step of the process.
8. Troubleshoot.

Please note that not every one of these steps will be relevant to every workshop. For example, the history of a particular craft might not be relevant or interesting to your participants. Likewise, instead of sectioning off a demonstration of techniques used, this might be done adjacent to the participants going through each step.

Safety precautions

When creating your workshop, it's essential that you risk-assess your activity and clearly detail:

- *Who is the course designed for?* Is it suitable for all ages? Can children safely do the course? Will children need adult supervision? Make sure to clearly state the target audience.

- *What tools and materials are required?* Are they sharp, dangerous? Always advise learners on best practice when using and storing tools and materials.

- *Safety equipment* – do you need to wear specific or protective clothing? For example, does the activity require eye protection? Make sure you give clear and detailed safety instructions.

- *Workshop space* – do learners need to work in a specific space or set-up? For example, do they need to be outdoors, or in a well-ventilated space? It's important to clearly identify the set-up required to complete the course safely.

Check whether the company is expecting you to have your own public liability insurance.

How will the event be communicated to employees and how will any risks in participating in the workshop or any practical advice be made clear? For example, if an activity is messy, will you or they provide aprons?

> **Tip**
>
> Attendees at events may not be aware that making can get messy! Ensure that participants are aware of any possible damage to clothes, especially if working with glue or other sticky materials, and provide aprons.

WORKSHOPS AT OTHER PUBLIC EVENTS

Makers and craftspeople are often invited to a range of other public events such as festivals, camps, fairs and other live demonstrations and workshops. The advice above will hold true for most public events, but with larger public events there are particular things to consider.

Samantha Razook

Samantha Razook is the founder and CEO of New York–based Curious Jane. Samantha started the company in 2009 as a summer camp for her own girls – and all girls – to be creative and inventive in a high-energy space. Curious Jane runs camps, classes and workshops year-round. Here she shares her top tips on running smooth workshops at a live event.

1. Be super-organized about supplies and set-up. Use clear bins, clearly labelled, and make sure any prep steps are done ahead of time. Once the event begins, your staff will be totally dedicated to the 'crafter' and it's amazing how many questions

some of them might have. It's also good to keep yourself free enough to chat with people – always learning and connecting.

2. If you are bringing any type of signage (branding, instructional, etc.), make sure it is clearly visible to participants. Once the event starts, anything below waist height or even shoulder height can be easily missed. In addition, any type of promotional signage on the table will take up workspace and be overlooked by participants.

3. Choose a super-simple project with fun materials and a bit of a 'wow' factor. Remember … you are a crafter/maker, but your participants may not be … and the project should be accessible and engaging. Choose a very simple project (with three to five steps) that is accessible to a range of ages and skills. A way to do this is to choose a project that has a core end-result but which can be elaborated on by more sophisticated crafters.

4. Have simple, printed how-tos with visual examples, all on one page. We call these our 'project placemats'. We print the instructions, making sure they are as visually driven as possible – more pictures, fewer words – and we laminate them. The project placemats can float around the table and be passed around for crafters to refer to. It's very difficult to have to explain the project live so you definitely want to have instructions that are obvious and easy to follow.

5. Know what to expect. Before the event, ask the host for an expected number of participants; ask for as much detail about your 'area' as possible, and find out whether you will have tables, tents and so on, or whether you should bring your own.

6. Choose lightweight supplies but bring extra. You don't want to be lugging heavy bins of supplies in and out of the event but you do want to have extra on hand. It's a balance.

7. Crowd control – plan in advance. If you are expecting crowds, have a plan to control the workspace at the tables and access to supplies. Make sure everyone has the chance to participate.

8. If it is a live event outdoor, remember the wind (and other weather) and plan for all eventualities.

9. Encourage participants to get creative and let their hands do the thinking.

7

Developing Your Brand and Marketing

In this chapter we will explore just some of the ways that you can develop your brand and market your products or services. For many makers and craftspeople the task of going out and marketing their products, developing a brand and sharing their creations can be exciting but also overwhelming. Technology has offered a proliferation of marketing opportunities to sell and market your products but has simultaneously created a number of challenges with regard to where to start and how much time to allocate.

If you are a small business, the temptation is to try to be everywhere and on every platform. This can create a phenomenon that some marketers have called 'tactical manoeuvre hell' where you're trying everything but simply not getting anywhere. In addition, for makers and craftspeople, trying to market their products on each and every available platform can leave little time for the very thing that is essential – making itself.

The key to successful marketing is to devise a simple strategy where the activity is:

- *achievable* – so you have the time to actually do the marketing work and not feel like you're always behind;
- *measurable* – there is little point in firing on all cylinders if you're not able to effectively measure whether that activity has been successful or not;
- Be conscious of your time and interrogate as often as possible whether the rewards reaped are a fair return on the investment of your time, and, in cases of advertising spend, money.

Building a brand strategy

The concept of 'brand' may be alien to many makers and craftspeople, but all businesses are emanating some kind of brand identity whether expressly or unknowingly. As demonstrated in Chapter 3: Understanding Your Customers, about personas, however individual we might think we are, the reality is that we likely fall into a number of category 'types' that are identifiable.

Branding is mostly synonymous with brand materials such as branded logos, style guides, colour palettes, packaging and so forth, but can extend to values, personality, tone of voice and more. Your brand is, however, about reflecting the personality of your business in a way that aligns with your audiences and community. Brand identity is the culmination of how your brand looks, feels and speaks to your audiences.

Your brand strategy will be made up of the following:

- your purpose (vision, mission and values)
- your message (brand voice, personality, tagline, value proposition)
- your brand identity (your logo, colour palette, typography).

While this might look like a lot of marketing language, these exercises can help you to come up with a set of rules that enable you to be consistent with all of your marketing – from visuals to social media.

There are a number of simple exercises to help you develop your branding, and we have included a number of templates in The Making a Living Programme. Most templates work from the same basics, which are to consider your mission and vision, to think about the language that you would use to describe you and your products, and to use a visual board to align colour and designs that you feel could reflect your brand.

Your brand style guide should include:

- your logo
- a colour palette (taking inspiration from photographs, paintings or more)
- typography
- illustration

- voice (house style for your written work)
- photography (house style for your imagery).

Once you have researched your brand values, and worked out your positioning and personas, the next step is to try to pull this into a visual identity that will start to mirror this. If you are working with a freelance designer to help you create a brand suite for you, they will probably ask you to share designs that you love, and designs that you hate, to try to understand broadly a look and feel of where you want to go.

Social media for arts, crafts and design

Social media platforms, as most of us have learned, are designed to suck you in and keep you there. While this is great for creating a sticky field of customers, these very same platforms can become a time-suck and preoccupation that is not necessarily helping you to build your business.

It's likely that you already have an Instagram account, a Facebook profile, a Twitter account or a few Pinterest boards. But having a social media account for your own personal use can be very different from managing social media for your brand.

Social media is important for outreach, solidifying a visual identity and connecting with the creative community. Few creative businesses could survive without it, so getting it right is vital.

There are many things to consider when creating your social media channels:

- handles
- which platforms to use
- content type and tone of voice
- brand aesthetic
- scheduling
- gaining followers
- trends and hashtags
- apps that help organize content.

Remember that social media is ever evolving, so it's important to stay up to date with trends and updates. It's also something that you'll become familiar with the more you use it. It's easy to begin, so we encourage you to start your social media journey right away.

OBJECTIVES AND AIMS

Having a clear understanding of the aim and objectives of your social media strategy will help you to plan it out. These might include one or more of the following strategies:

- gathering opinions
- providing trust signals
- driving sales
- driving awareness
- driving click-throughs
- developing community: around a specific topic/area of interest
- developing community: informing and supporting a specific audience
- responding personally or as a business to a political question or a global event.

Social media can bring a lot of value to your brand, but it can also be a lot to take on. Be mindful of what you hope to gain from your social media, write it down, and centre your strategy on this.

First things first. Before you start posting any content, you'll need an account. In order to create one, you'll need a **handle** that will be associated with your brand.

The handle is how your brand will be discovered, tagged and recognized. It is essentially your username, and on many social media platforms it follows the @ (at) symbol. For example, Yodomo's handle on Instagram is @yodomo.co.

Your handle should be consistent across the various platforms you use, and it should be easily recognizable. If the handle you want to use is taken, try different variations of it. If we follow the example of the company we incorporated in Chapter 2, if the business is called Amy's Crafts, and @amyscrafts is taken, then you would try @amys.crafts,

@amys_crafts, or other combinations that will properly reflect your brand name and still be recognizable.

Once you've established that your handle is available, it's time to create your accounts.

CHOOSING THE RIGHT SOCIAL MEDIA PLATFORMS

You might have a personal Instagram account or Facebook profile, or else you may already use Pinterest for inspiration or Twitter to be in the know. You've likely watched your share of videos on YouTube, have connected with colleagues on LinkedIn, and you might have already become an addict of TikTok's addictive algorithm. If you have the time, it would be great to have brand accounts on all of them, but running a brand is time-consuming enough without adding extra channels that constantly need updating. Consider how much time you're willing to spend on each platform, and whether having an account with each is worthwhile. It may be more effective to choose a smaller number of accounts and run those as strategically as possible.

Here we will quickly run through some of the biggest social media platforms, scheduling tools, paid-for advertising and more. This is an *extremely* fast-moving area, so we advise you to do a deeper dive in The Making a Living Programme where you can keep up to date with tips and advice from fellow makers and craftspeople.

INSTAGRAM

Instagram is ideal for cementing your brand aesthetic, finding potential customers and networking with like-minded individuals. For makers, it's something few can do without. You can now sell directly on Instagram, which makes it even more worthwhile to sign up. It's also a great way to stay connected with the community of designers, makers and creatives, keeping track of trends and being a part of bigger movements.

We recommend starting on Instagram and, to begin with, posting every other day. Reach out to your friends and family to give you a follow to start off your audience base, follow like-minded businesses and accounts, and research other brands similar to yours to see what type of content works best. Every audience and every brand are different, so what works for others may not work for you, but trying out a few different approaches will give you a good sense of the type of content, time of publication and tags that work best for you.

PINTEREST

Pinterest is a virtual pinboard that lets you pin images and links from anywhere on the internet, making mood boards or other visual planning efforts easy. Highly visual and flexible in content type, it also provides links for each post, giving your website great backlinks that are important for search engine optimization (SEO) and making it easier for your audiences to click through to whatever you're selling, sharing or raising awareness for. It's also a good home for popular 'how-to' creative projects.

As a creative business, Pinterest is a good platform to be on, and it's easy to pin content with a few clicks using the Pinterest browser extension.

FACEBOOK

Facebook remains a popular social media platform that offers unparalleled opportunities for online networking. Although its younger audiences are declining, it is still important in reaching specific communities both locally and around the world.

You can share Facebook posts to your own friends' list or in groups that you are a part of, some of which can reach audiences in the thousands. Because of this, we would advise creating a Facebook page for your business. Even if you post infrequently, having it means you'll be discoverable on a major platform.

YOUTUBE

If you have video content, then creating a YouTube account is a must. As YouTube content is usually evergreen (meaning it can have value even years after it's uploaded), and because it's used more to surface and share videos than to network, there is less urgency to constantly add new content.

YouTube is also the second most popular search engine after Google, so having a YouTube channel with videos relevant to your practice will enable you to be discoverable by a much wider audience.

Videos can also be monetized via YouTube, so if your videos become popular enough, it will provide an additional revenue stream for you.

We recommend creating a YouTube channel even if, so far, you have only a single video. You can add anything from free content to previews of paid-for content, and there's no pressure to constantly post new videos.

TIKTOK

TikTok videos are one minute in length or shorter, and there are many functions in-app that you can use in order to upgrade your video content, such as background music or stitching videos together.

Videos can accrue thousands of views in minutes, easily bringing your brand or practice to the attention of many. Its algorithm also surfaces videos from months before, so, in terms of upkeep, it is currently placed somewhere between Instagram and YouTube for how often you should be adding content. If you have video content already, or if you want to start making some and take advantage of a new platform, we suggest creating an account.

TWITTER

Twitter is great for sharing updates, images, memes and small bits of text, but it does require constant upkeep and posting. It's also great for sharing links, as it provides backlinks for SEO purposes and can help with click-throughs. If you have the time and resources to maintain a Twitter account, it would be a great idea to have one, especially if you anticipate others tagging you in Tweets. If, however, you are likely not to have the time to consistently update your Twitter, this is one account that you may want to pass over.

OTHER PLATFORMS TO CONSIDER

There are several other social media platforms that might be interesting for your particular practice. Depending on your expertise and resources, joining some of these may also be a good idea. A few other popular ones include:

- *Snapchat* This remains a popular platform among younger people, with over 250 million daily active users in 2021, surpassing Twitter and on a par with LinkedIn. You could promote your business or brand by posting stories similar to those made with Instagram, and if your core demographic is between 18 and 30, this might be worth investing time into.

- *Medium* This is the place to surface longer-form prose. It's a place where you can share thoughts and how-tos, and let a different audience know all about your brand and what you've learned in creating it. If you have a website, Medium is also great for SEO, and you can publish the same content on your own blog as you might on Medium.

- *LinkedIn* This is great for connecting with businesses or those who represent businesses. It's where you can find those with skills that might suit your needs while also letting others know about your particular skillset or your brand. It's also useful if you target corporate clients with your workshops.

- *Reddit* This hosts very specific communities (or 'subreddits') which have their own rules for what can be posted. Communities cater directly to specific interests or needs (e.g. more than 300,000 users participate in the Embroidery subreddit). We suggest you browse and see what is posted in specific communities first in order to get a good overview of how they work.

- *The Dots* This is a fantastic way to share creative projects you've worked on, either for yourself or for other organizations. It's a place where you can surface the events you hold, the skillset you have, and where you can connect with others who can either help you with your brand or who may be interested in seeing what you have to offer.

SCHEDULING

Thanks to automation you can now schedule your social media posts days, or even weeks, ahead of time. This is useful if you want to work on social media in a block of time, and don't want to be interrupted from your workflow in order to post new content to your feeds.

Even if you plan only posting live, it's important to consider when you should post, in order to gain the right type of traffic or earn more impressions. Consider where your target demographic is located, and the time zones they're in. It wouldn't make sense to post something at 3am BST when you're trying to reach a UK audience. Similarly, it may be good to find when posts are shared the most and avoid this time in order to avoid too much competition. Have a play around with scheduling along with content type in order to determine what works best for your brand.

In terms of ways to schedule your social media content, there are several applications you can use (see below), some of which are free and some of which have a monthly fee. Other free scheduling tools can be found on the channels themselves, such as on Facebook and Pinterest.

Because Facebook also owns Instagram, you'll be able to use Facebook's **Business Suite** in order to schedule Instagram posts, too. For Twitter, you can use **Tweetdeck** and YouTube, and LinkedIn also allows you to schedule posts.

Third-party applications for scheduling include the following:

- *Hootsuite* This is a one-stop shop for most of the above-mentioned channels, plus tools to help manage ads and analytics.

- *Tailwind* A specific tool for Instagram and Pinterest, this gives optimized times for scheduling as well as in-app tools to create content.

- *Later* This is used for Instagram, Pinterest and TikTok, Later can be used not only to schedule posts but also for Instagram Stories. Its calendar view also makes it easy to keep track of scheduled posts.

- *Sprout Social* This covers all the social media channels you might want to maintain, covering everything from Twitter to YouTube; a lot of major organizations use it.

There are many other ways to schedule your content, and other apps might do the trick better for you. The benefits of these third-party apps are in their convenience, but also in the hashtag suggestions, content suggestions and other prompts that may help you to produce more effective content.

TRENDS AND HASHTAGS

Keeping relevant with your content will gain you a bigger following and better outreach, so it's important to be in the know with **trends**. The best way to gain an overview of what's popular is to immerse yourself in social media. This will help you to get a better understanding of what your audience may want to see because you'll also be an audience member.

Keeping tabs on social media will also help you zero in on phenomena that happen exclusively on social media, such as memes. For example, during the 2021 US presidential inauguration, Senator Bernie Sanders sitting with his arms crossed and wearing a pair of cosy mittens became a widely shared image across all social media platforms. This image became a meme, where individuals Photoshopped him into various film stills, events and situations. In a stroke of inspiration, maker Tobey King posted a crocheted version of this meme, which in itself went viral, ending up raising $40,000 for Meals on Wheels America when sold via auction.

Keeping up with trends does not necessarily lead to virality, but it does mean that more of your audience will engage with your posts if it's relevant.

Hashtags can also help with understanding what's on trend. On Twitter, for example, you can look at currently trending tags. Pinterest also lets you find trends according to region or country.

For other platforms, trends are not so simply surfaced, but there are ways besides spending time on each app to discover what hashtags are being used. For Instagram, you can search hashtags to see how many posts have been tagged, and how recently it's been used. You can see the top posts with that tag to see how competitive that tag might be, and you can also follow certain tags to see whenever someone else posts using that tag.

PAID ADVERTISEMENTS ON SOCIAL MEDIA

Paid advertisements on social media can offer more click-throughs, increase sales and gain a following. It might be a good idea to allocate some of your budget for sponsored posts in order to quickly increase the number of followers. This may be important as a strong social media following can indicate a trustworthy brand for some customers.

Be aware that this can quickly get pricey if you're not budgeting it out carefully, so make sure you're keeping a close eye on marketing spend on social media. It can also skew data if you're trying to find the sweet spot in terms of content type for your brand, so we suggest first testing the waters to see what is well liked by your followers before paying for sponsored posts.

INFLUENCERS

Influencers have become a big part of social media marketing, and there are influencers useful for all kinds of business – even crafts and making. These influencers can cater directly to the audience you're after, and they might be easier to reach than you think.

The influencers in your life

There are several levels of influencers, all dependent on how many followers an account has. But even if an account has a mere few hundred followers, this could be something that starts a buzz.

We all have those people in our lives whose advice on products or brands we take seriously. With this in mind, you can look at your direct contacts, including friends and family, in order to ask them for help by posting about your brand or your products.

You can also give them something you've made in exchange for a post. You never know who they'll be able to reach. This type of outreach is great for building an organic following, starting off small but with huge potential to continue growing.

Paid-for influencer marketing

If you're looking for more impact, there are many paid-for influencer networks or collaborations you can explore. Although they tend to be pricey, and there's no guarantee that you'll be able to make a return with sales, chances are you'll gain at least some sales, and you'll be able to retain some followers from this.

If you'd like to explore paid-for influencer marketing, be sure to research the type of person you want to be associated with your brand, as well as the platform they'll promote your products on. Start by looking at the hashtags associated with your products, and seeing what some of the top posts are. YouTube videos with lots of views or channels with lots of subscribers are also a good avenue to explore.

Public relations (PR)

In the age of social media the value of other media is often overlooked, but a well-placed article in the right magazine can not only help you find new audiences but also acts as a trust signal to your customers if they can see you've been featured. Also most media outlets will now also share content simultaneously on their own social media channels so you might get increased reach here.

Approaching journalists is not as scary as you might think. Collate journalist names who are writing in areas that your products or services fit into. You might be able to follow journalists on their own social media channels and raise awareness of your products and services initially that way. Most editorial teams are very pushed for time, so approach them with a pitch that makes it as easy as possible for them to run with it. For example, do some of the homework for them, explain a market trend and show them how your work is relevant to their readers or audiences.

There are more tips on approaching journalists in The Making a Living Programme as well as a template for a press release.

Partnerships

Creating good partnerships is a really effective and inexpensive way to build your audiences. Also, you'll be pleasantly surprised as to how many businesses are up for collaborations and partnerships, especially with creative businesses, so don't be afraid to ask.

The advantages of partnerships include:

- You can reach new audiences with your products or workshops.
- You can benefit from marketing on their social media platforms.
- You can position your brand by aligning it with like-minded brands.

Key to a good partnership is a clear understanding of what the implications are for each party. Make sure that you have a written agreement stipulating what each business will be bringing to the table. For example: '*The influencer* commits to sharing the designed assets on social media platforms (Instagram, Facebook and Pinterest) during the given period in return for *the product*.'

Eli Wislocka

Craft business Love & Salvage regularly use partnerships with maker influencers to bring their kits to life. Its founder, **Eli Wislocka**, gives her top tips on how to structure a happy partnership.

I decided that I would develop a partnership strategy and spend my money and energy cultivating partnerships instead of paid advertising. I found advertising a big financial commitment that I couldn't really get my head round, whereas partnerships were simple, friendly, organic ways to grow my audience. One of the first things I did was accept that this is not a 'free' strategy per se, as to grow quickly you need to be prepared to pay, and I would be paying by giving away products.

I started looking for like-minded individuals who had a similar audience to mine, and to begin with I sent them a message telling them all about my business and asking them if they would like a free gift in exchange for sharing my product on their profile.

I made sure I started with people with small audiences of around 10,000, who were local to me, because I wanted local customers and business and felt that they were much more likely to support my business. I also accepted that some people would enthusiastically accept my gift and then be a little bit tight with their side of the bargain – I think that about 40 per cent of partnerships are a bit disappointing in this way. Then slowly, as my audience grows, I am seeking partnerships with people with bigger audiences.

I have found that the partnerships not only give my business wider reach and more sales, but I get fantastic content for social media, too.

Other marketing tips and advice

MAKE TIME-LAPSE VIDEOS OF YOUR MAKING

There is something very satisfying about seeing something created from beginning to end. Make videos of yourself engaging with your practice, and show off what you can do. This will also encourage others to get creative and try out your demonstrations. You can make simple time-lapse videos using just your smartphone.

For both iPhones and Androids, set up your phone in a place where you'll be able to capture your hands doing what they do best: engaging in skillful techniques in order to make something creative. Once set in place, open your camera app and go to the time-lapse function.

Press the record button and start creating. Once you're done, press 'stop' and your video will be automatically saved. You may have to crop the beginning and end of the video by going into 'edit' to take out the parts where you press 'record' and 'stop'.

SHARE ACCOLADES

If you win a prize, are invited to take part in a group exhibition or else have simply mastered a new technique, share the good news with your followers. Social media is where many people keep up with news on those they follow, and good news helps promote engagement.

SHARE PERSONAL JOURNEYS

People want to know that they're supporting a genuine person as opposed to a corporation. They want to be a part of your journey of growth. This is why it's a good idea to be candid about your successes and struggles and to tell a story about why you're doing what you're doing. This provides further trust signals for followers, ensuring them that you're the right person they should be buying from.

Once you've gained a bit of a following, you can promote your brand with contests via social media. This may involve followers sharing a specific post or tagging a friend in order to win one of your products. You can also consider collaborating with other brands in order to offer winners a bundle of different prizes, where entry into the competition would involve a follow and like for each participating brand.

BUILD UP YOUR TRUST SIGNALS

As a new business competing in a busy global marketplace you will want to quickly establish some trust signals that lead new customers to consider you a trustworthy company to buy from. Trust signals might include customer reviews, client testimonials, professional body memberships and more.

Trust signals can be shared on your website, your marketing materials and more. They have become very important in the world of e-commerce as customers might land on your website and not know anything about you, so any positive indications you can give them that you are a trustworthy company might make the difference between a sale or no sale.

Trust signals might include:

- *Client testimonials or 'social proof'* This type of trust signal includes everything from customer reviews to word-of-mouth recommendations. Try to capture reviews as widely as possible even if this feels terrifying at first.

- *Trust by association* Aesop, the ancient Greek storyteller, said, 'A man is known by the company he keeps', and this is also true of new businesses. Are there partners you are working with who are trusted within your community or by your target market? Use your partnerships and collaborations with more established brands to garner this trust by association.

- *Trusted membership organizations* Are you a member of a trusted crafts or maker organization? Have you come through a well-known degree for arts, crafts or design? These can all act as trust signals to a potential customer. If you have a professional qualification in your area of craftsmanship, ensure that this is clearly stated for customers to see.

- *Media reviews* Have your products been reviewed in a magazine or newspaper? Getting someone else to say your product or service is brilliant is a much more powerful way than you saying it yourself. Take out the best part of the article and use it across your marketing.

- *Funders* Have you received grant funding from established public bodies or arts organizations? Most funders encourage you to share their logo on your website, social media and printed materials and can be a power trust signal to customers.

- *Prizes* Have you won any prizes for your work or received any commendations? Use these on your website, social media or other marketing materials to demonstrate your expertise in a certain area.

- *Clear contact details* Customers like to know that they're dealing with a genuine company, so any information that you can supply to prove you are a business will help them. For example, if you're registered at Companies House as a limited company you could put your company number here and a physical address.

Exercise

1. Develop a simple brand book to help you talk visually about your crafts and maker business.
2. Write down which social media platforms you feel are the best home for your business, and where the right audiences will be.
3. Set up social media handles for the platforms you will be using.
4. Create a simple content planner and be realistic about how often you will post online – consistency is better than a big push initially and then leaving it for weeks.
5. Create a database of influencers and journalists, and build up this list as your business develops and grows.
6. Use the templates available in The Making a Living Programme to help you develop the following:

   - a brand book
   - a style guide
   - trust signals
   - press releases
   - a content planner.

8

Managing Your Accounts and Tax

For many makers and craftspeople a business will evolve organically from that first sale of a handmade item at a market through to an online sale on a website. If you're not used to running business accounts, getting to grips with basic accounting is a really important step for any small business, from a sole trader through to a limited company.

There are not many people who really enjoy the prospect of financial administration or thinking about tax, but it is really essential to try to grasp the basics of business accounting, to understand your profit margins and your tax liabilities, to give you peace of mind and feel in control of your finances.

Each country has its own tax and accounting legislation, so this chapter will cover the principles of basic accounting, consider accounting in the context specifically for crafts and making businesses, and help you ensure that your finances run smoothly across the year.

CREATING A BESPOKE BUSINESS ACCOUNT

One of the most important things to consider when starting a business is where your sales income is going to be deposited. As a sole trader you might just have your payments going into your main bank account, but having a separate bank account for your business can really help you to understand the impact of expenses against the business, help you see your overall taxable income at a glance, and overall just not get confused with other income and expenditure in a personal account.

You might want to stick to your current bank, but there is a suite of new banks targeting small businesses and considering the specific needs of small businesses. The new banks, such as Tide, Starling and

ANNA Money, have positioned themselves as offering a new kind of banking that understands the specific needs of small businesses, with some even specifically looking at the needs of creative entrepreneurs, so do look at these new options.

ANNA

Lily Smith put together these handy budget-building tips for ANNA Money, reproduced with its kind permission.

Why is budgeting important?

It may sound obvious, but the main reason why small businesses fail is because they lose control of their finances. So if you want your business to last, you need to take care of your finances every step of the way.

You can do this by creating a business budget, which outlines the current state of your finances (including income and expenses) as well as your long-term financial goals. You'll also use your business budget to make sure you can meet your current financial commitments (and have money for future commitments if you want to grow your business). Business planning doesn't have to be complicated – but it's important to get everything down in writing before you begin. Your budget will play a key role in making sensible financial decisions for your business, so it should be one of the first tasks you tackle. Then, throughout the year, you can monitor your budget and, if things change, you can account for them when you make your next plan.

How do I put together a business budget?

Decide on your budgeting tools. If you're just starting out and want to keep your costs down, there are plenty of free business budgeting templates online. If you do invest in some accounting software, it will often have a built in budgeting tool – so take full advantage!

Look at your figures

Now you need to account for all your incomings and outgoings so you can balance your books. Make a list of all of your fixed costs (the costs that remain the same regardless of how much business you do – such as lease or rental payments, insurance and interest payments) and a list of your variable costs. Variable costs are those that change as your income changes – so things like materials, travel expenses, light and heating costs. Everything you spend money on needs to be accounted for so that you can create an accurate estimate of your income and outgoings for the year.

Monitor regularly

Now it's time for the fun (we may be stretching the definition of fun) part: you'll need to monitor your budget against the actual figures and investigate any variances (that's the difference between the budget and the actual cost). Investigating the variances can highlight what you've done well so you can do it again, or what you've done badly – to help you avoid doing that again.

You can create a budget for the year, but if you're a seasonal business (e.g. an ice cream shop) or just starting up, then a month-by-month or quarterly analysis is going to give you a much more accurate idea of how your business is doing. Remember to keep your budget realistic and conservative – estimate low in terms of income, and high in terms of expenses, so you reduce the chance of running out of money.

An important part of business budgeting is setting your fees and prices – it can be a bit of a minefield, so do your research. If you set your prices low to undercut competitors, you could be left scratching around for a profit. When you're budgeting your income, make sure you build into your profit margin the costs of delivering your products or services. That might be tricky to estimate if you're in retail or selling a service that combines materials and labour. If you provide a service, it's a bit easier to budget for your time and expertise.

One word of advice: be aware of your competitors, but don't build your prices or rates on theirs. You don't know all the ins and outs of their accounts, and your budget might be totally different!

What costs do businesses have?

These can be divided simply into your fixed costs and your variable costs. Your fixed costs include things like your rent or mortgage, any business rates, your phone and broadband bills – basically, the regular costs you know you'll be paying every month. If you pay business insurance, or need professional indemnity insurance because your business offers professional advice (like an accountant or lawyer), then these are fixed costs, too.

Your variable costs include all your other business expenses – from travel and marketing costs to materials and labour. You can read more about what counts as a business expense at https://anna. money/blog/guides/how-to-organise-your-receipts-for-taxes/ Variable costs are costs that change as the quantity of the goods or services you provide change. That's why it's so important to keep an eye on your variable costs as your business grows.

How do I keep on top of my cash flow?

Before we answer that, you need to be clear what your cash flow is. Cash flow is the total amount of cash being transferred into and out of your business. Businesses can fail even if they're profitable on paper – if they don't get paid on time, they can quickly run into debt. Look after your cash flow by staying on top of your billing – the money that's owed to you after you've provided goods or services. Try to collect payments as soon as you can, using online payments if possible as they'll reach your account quicker than a cheque or a cash payment you pay in at a bank counter.

Be aware of your credit terms – if you have 30 days' interest-free credit before a payment is due, pay towards the end of the 30 days so you have as much time as possible to accrue the money you need. Take advantage of credit terms from your suppliers, making careful notes of every due date so you're never charged late fees. You might find it easier on your cash flow if you ask for deposits on larger contracts, or stage payments to spread your upfront costs.

If you're a new business, you can look after your cash flow by leasing rather than buying assets. If you need an expensive piece of equipment to do your job, monthly rental payments will put your cash flow under less pressure than a large one-off payment. A lot of people also take advantage of a business credit card to delay costs – some cards offer two-month payment terms, which extends the amount of time you have to pay your bills while you're waiting for payments to come in.

Setting your own credit terms and payment requirements is important, too. Don't feel you have to offer 30 days' credit when you're first in business – check whether your customers will accept one week. If you're only asking for payment after the job is done (like most tradespeople), then payment should be immediate – as soon as you've completed the work. Think of retail, where payment terms are immediate! Then as you grow and your cash flow becomes more established, you can offer better payment terms to offset your competitors.

What tools can I use to help plan my budget?

The most useful tool when you create your business budget is a simple budgeting template – budgeting templates tend to have exhaustive lists of all expense categories, so you can account for everything. There's some excellent budgeting software out there; you might not want to pay for anything extra when you're starting out, but it's a good investment and using software makes budgeting less of a faff.

Remember, your time is money – especially as a small business owner! One useful trick is looking at the published accounts of larger companies in the same industry at Companies House, so you can see the types of expenses they incur that you may have overlooked. Also, don't be afraid to ask an accountant for professional advice at any stage of your budget planning – it could save you money in the long run.

Can I plan a budget in Excel?

Absolutely – Excel is an easy-to-use tool for business budgeting, and it's an industry standard for all accountants. That means you can easily share your budget with your accountant when you're ready to do your tax return. Just make sure you use a decent Excel template for your budget. There are plenty of them online that you can download for free.

Getting paid

As a maker or craftsperson you might have a number of different ways that you are paid – for example:

- cash or card payments at a crafts market or maker fair
- card payment online – via Stripe, PayPal and so on
- card or cash payments for physical workshops
- card payment for online courses.

With each of these transactions there might be hidden fees from the card payment provider or online payment system, and documenting all of these transactions can quickly become quite complicated. There are some things to look out for:

Shopify will pay out into your account in batches and its fees are taken off at source. You may need to break this down further in your bookkeeping so that it is clear what is sales income and what is the fees you have paid.

Cash taken at a crafts market or fair can easily slip into petty cash and be spent on drinks or lunch. Remember to try to accurately record each sale, as over the long term it will give you more accurate data on your sales, and the more sales income you can log in your accounts, the more options may be available to you as you grow.

If you can get your head around Excel or Google Sheets, you might be able to keep a close eye on your accounts through a simple Income and Expenditure spreadsheet. We have created a basic template available in The Making a Living Programme.

There are now also a number of low-cost digital accounting software platforms such as **Xero** or **QuickBooks** that are really useful for small businesses, as they can use them not only to run the accounting software but to generate invoices as well. In addition, many of these software providers will run free-of-charge online courses to help you to get to grips with the system.

Take advantage of these free training courses as many of them also include basic accounting courses as part of their packages. Even if you decide to use an accountant or a bookkeeper, having the knowledge of basic accounting will put you in good stead as you grow.

Talking about money

If you've not run a small business before, getting comfortable with talking about money is the first challenge you need to overcome. Starting out, often your customers can be friends and family, and charging for your work might feel awkward or uncomfortable. A good way to start is to break down your pricing (getting to grips with how your time, your materials and other costs all contribute to the final purchase price), as this may help you communicate the value of your work to others.

You will also want to get to grips with some basic accounting principles and terms, as these will help you as you grow. Whatever the size of your business now, don't put your head in the sand if you hate financial administration. Investing some time now into learning the basics will pay dividends, literally, in the future and save a lot of stress.

Pricing your products

At the outset it can be too easy for small businesses to consume everyday costs personally and not surface these carefully. The problem with this is that you can get a false view on how your business is doing, and it may cause you to under-price your work or possibly pay too much tax.

Working with a simple spreadsheet to calculate your costs will help you better understand your costs, and possibly where you might reduce these, and will also help you to price your work fairly, ensuring that you have a profit margin.

Consider all the costs associated with your business, which might include:

- *Making time* Some makers like to make it clear to customers the length of time it takes to make an item, in order to warrant a specific price tag. Give yourself an hourly rate and ensure that your time is covered. If it takes five hours to make 30 items, then split this cost out accordingly.

- *Materials* Consider all of the materials that go into making your handmade product and calculate backwards to get to a cost per item.

- *Overheads* Consider what other costs are involved, such as printing, transport of items, and so on.

- *Packaging* How much does it cost to package your item (for e-commerce)?

- *Shipping* Many customers now expect free shipping, so you will have to account for this in your pricing strategy.

You will also want to take into account that you might want a trade retailer or gallery to sell your handmade goods directly while ensuring that your wholesale price still allows a profit margin. Ideally, you should calculate a 'wholesale' price and a 'retail' price.

There are some formulas that might help you with pricing your handmade goods. Etsy suggests applying the following formulas to help you get to your wholesale and retail price points:

Wholesale Price = (Materials + Time Spent / Labour + Overhead) × 2

Retail Price = Wholesale Price × 2 [Etsy suggests that you can choose your multiplier here]

There are other makers who work with different formulas, for example:

Materials + Time Spent = Base Price

Base Price × 2 = Retail Price

Try using The Making a Living Programme pricing calculator to help you get to a realistic retail and wholesale price for your work. It is much easier to add in a generous profit margin at the beginning and give yourself some room for manoeuvre if you decide to offer any price promotions in the future.

Getting to the right price point for your target audience can sometimes be challenging, and if you're worried about a retail price coming out too high, then consider the following:

- Are there costs that you can reduce through buying in bulk or changing materials?

- What are your competitors charging? Can you see how they're able to charge a price lower than yours?

- Can you more clearly communicate to your customers the time, materials and other costs that have gone into making this product to help them understand the price point?

Is there any value in underselling your work? Can you calculate the lifetime value of a customer if they are more likely to come back at a lower price point?

Pricing your online courses

Pricing your products can actually be a simpler task than pricing your online courses or workshops because there is a physical element to it, and material costs to be able to point to. With online courses, pricing becomes even more complicated because pricing digital content is hard.

The biggest learning management platforms which host online courses, such as Thinkific and Teachable, are united in saying that you should try not to devalue your online course content just because it is digital and maintain a value that is representative of your skill and experience.

There are many stages to creating an online course, and that's not to mention all the years you have accumulated the knowledge to be able to share your skills online in the first place.

One thing that makes it very difficult to price online content is that there is a lot of free digital content available. This is where leaning on your experience and trust signals is really important to demonstrate the value of your online course and why learning from you represents more value than YouTube, for example.

Both Thinkific and Teachable have created some useful structures to help you price your online content, so do have a look at these to try and gauge a price point that feels right to you.

Pricing a live workshop

Hosting a live workshop requires your time during the workshop, preparation, costs of materials, sometimes transport costs and more. Pricing live workshops can be tricky, especially as some organizations will approach you with a set price. Approach pricing your live workshop in exactly the same way, considering your time, your expertise and your material costs before agreeing to a set fee.

Don't be afraid to explain to an organizer why you would be unable to provide a workshop for a specific fee. You can also suggest that they cover material costs and make it clear what your workshop fee is, as this will clarify the cost of your time versus the combined cost where the materials really start to eat into a profit margin.

Companies who book creative workshops as part of a wellbeing initiative will often have a per head budget, and it's useful to ask them upfront what this budget is so that you can give a number of options. It might be that the workshop they approach you about is not going to work within their budget, but there might be a version of it that is possible once you're clear on the parameters of the budget.

Increasingly, companies asking for creative workshops are also interested in sustainability and reuse of materials, so any workshop you create for them where employees are reusing materials will evidently bring down overall costs. However, you should maintain your workshop fee as this reflects the value of your expertise and the learning you are bringing to the table.

One thing to take into consideration when working with corporate bookings is that some businesses will take some time to pay your invoice and won't begin to process it until the workshop has taken place. Where possible, ask the company if they will consider 50 per cent payment on contract or MOU (memorandum of understanding) and 50 per cent on delivery to ensure that any upfront costs can be covered off quite quickly.

Learning to negotiate

Many people find the process of negotiating embarrassing or stressful, but it's a necessary part of business. For more crafts businesses negotiation often comes into play when negotiating the price of a workshop.

Having a clear pricing structure at your fingertips can really help you when negotiating. Before you draw up a pricing structure, try to consider the time involved with the activity and the materials involved. Where possible, do your research and understand the competition.

Where possible, too, ask the potential client to lead with what they pay for workshops. You might find that they have a structure in place that dictates the kind of a workshop you can deliver within that budget.

If the budget seems very low, try to communicate to them why you feel this to be the case. For example, if the budget only just covers your materials, then explain this to them and that you're not able to work for free. Most businesses are understanding once they have a better understanding of what is entailed.

Also, don't be afraid to turn down a low-paid opportunity. You want your time to be valued, and sometimes it's better to walk away than to work for nothing.

Once you've determined a fee, be sure to get this in writing as soon as possible along with a clear indication of:

- price (including whether VAT is added to this)
- date and time
- number of participants (including additional costs if more people take part)
- travel costs (whether included or added on)
- cancellation fee – this is really important as it can cost you money if you buy in materials and the workshop gets cancelled.

Tax

The tax implications for selling your products will vary depending on where you live and what you're selling. Whether you are operating as a sole trader or a limited company you are running a business and therefore there are tax implications on your income.

UK tax checklist

- Are you a sole trader or a limited company?
- Have you registered with HMRC?
- Has your turnover exceeded the VAT threshold?

US tax checklist

- If you're self-employed and selling online, read tax tips from Turbo Tax here: https://turbotax.intuit.com/tax-tips/self-employment-taxes/tax-tips-for-selling-your-handmade-items-online
- If you're running as a business, read tax tips from Turbo Tax here: https://turbotax.intuit.com/tax-tips/self-employment-taxes/selling-on-etsy-your-taxes/L27I196Wu

Many makers and craftspeople will have portfolio careers – that is to say, creating income from a number of different revenue streams from varying careers – so understanding the tax implications if you are self-employed for part of your income and employed for the rest can easily become complicated.

When to get an accountant

If you're anxious about running the accounts for your business, or your business is growing quickly, then you might want to consider paying out for an accountant or bookkeeper. As a small business owner, one of the most important calculations to make is whether the time spent worrying about tax return deadlines is worth the cost of an accountant and/or a bookkeeper.

Exercise

Use our templates to help you to create:
- a basic cash flow
- prices for your finished products that take into account your time and materials.

9

Customer Relations

As a crafts and making business you will be dealing with customers wherever you might meet them, whether that is through selling handmade goods in person at a market, selling to them online or teaching them in a workshop. Building up a network of happy customers is one of the best things you can do to grow your business as word-of-mouth recommendation is still one of the most powerful marketing tools.

You need to take your relationship with your customers seriously, so you will need to develop a customer service strategy and a customer relationship management system, whether that is in a spreadsheet or an online tool.

A good place to start when thinking about your relationship with your customers is to consider what you appreciate when you are the customer yourself. What are the things that other companies and service providers do that make you feel valued and understood as a customer?

In this chapter we'll break down the different customer intersection points and consider each of these separately, and also look at how to create an ongoing relationship with your customers for long-term benefit and, hopefully, repeat sales and recommendations.

Customer care when selling directly

Before selling at a crafts market, fair or other retail point, try to think about all the ways in which you can add value to your customers beyond the sale itself. For example, if you're selling a terrarium, is it clear how the customer should care for it once they get it home? Could you be pointing your customer to free online content that will help them look after their terrarium? What should they do if they have any problems with their terrarium? Are you contactable if they have further questions?

Also be clear on your returns policy, especially if it is a local event. Having a clear returns policy can sometimes make the difference between a sale and a no sale, especially in the case of gifting.

Try to put yourself in the place of the customer and consider their thought processes about the item that they're about to purchase? If you were buying this item, would you be wondering how to care for it – whether it's machine washable, can go into a dishwasher, and so on? Even if you work with materials often and their care is second nature to you, remember that your customers may not be aware of the specific actions they need to take to look after an item.

Consider creating a special care label with full instructions to include in your bag as the customer leaves your stall or shop.

Customers services and online sales

You might discover with your e-commerce store that customers assume that you are a much bigger operation than you are, depending on whether you are operating as a standalone brand or working under your own name. Online customers are now so used to having to deal with bots and other automated customer services that you might find that they use language that feels unfriendly or demanding. If you can quickly respond as a human being, and as the maker or founder of the company, customers will often become more empathetic straight away and you are quickly able to resolve a query or a complaint.

If a customer is looking to return an item, it will help you enormously to have a clear **returns and refunds policy** and to ensure that this is clearly signposted. In your returns and refunds policy ensure that you clarify:

- whether or not you accept returns;
- the time frame in which you can accept a return;
- who will pay for the cost of return postage for any items that are sent back to you.

With returns and refunds, you should also check statutory legislation that covers consumer rights, as these will typically trump any returns and refunds policy you establish.

Under the **UK Consumer Rights Act 2015** (www.legislation.gov.uk/ukpga/2015/15/contents/enacted), consumers 'may be entitled to a refund, replacement, repair or compensation where goods are faulty or not as described'. UK government guidance states that you do not have to refund a customer if they:

- knew an item was faulty when they bought it;
- damaged an item by trying to repair it themselves or getting someone else to do it (though they may still have the right to a repair, replacement or partial refund);
- no longer want an item (e.g. because it's the wrong size or colour) unless they bought it without seeing it.

There is a useful guide to writing a returns policy on the UK government-funded Business Companion website (www.businesscompanion.info) which offers free legal advice for businesses. It recommends that your refunds policy includes your legal rights, plus any additional policies you might want to add to protect your customers.

Here is sample copy for a returns and refunds policy:

Your legal rights:

When you buy goods from a business, in law you have a number of rights as a consumer. These include the right to claim a refund, replacement, repair and/or compensation where the goods are faulty or misdescribed.

Our policy:

In addition to your legal rights, we also allow you to return goods if you simply change your mind. Please return the unused goods to us with the original till receipt within 14 days and we will offer you an exchange or a credit note.

How to deal with complaints or queries

What every small business fears more than anything else is a complaint or a difficult query from a customer. If you get a complaint from a customer, the best thing is to take stock: don't be tempted to fire back a defensive email straight away; instead take a step back and put yourself in the customer's shoes.

It might be that you need some time to work out the whereabouts of an order, or to work out what has happened with a particular product before going back to the customer. It's useful to have a standardized 'holding' email that politely states that you have seen their message and that you are dealing with it. As you grow, you may want to set up an automated email as an out of office that explains how quickly the customer can expect a response.

The collective ThinkJar reports that it is six to seven times more expensive to attract a new customer than it is to retain an existing one. Pick your battles and consider how important word of mouth is, especially if you're growing your business. When communicating with customers be mindful of the following:

- If satisfied by the customer experience, 73 per cent of consumers will recommend a brand to others, and 46 per cent say they will trust that brand's products and services above all others (*Source*: SDL Global CX).

- Some 76 per cent of consumers say they view customer service as the true test of how much a company values them (*Source*: Aspect Consumer Experience Survey).

LOST AND DAMAGED PACKAGES

One of the biggest issues that craftspeople and makers have to contend with is the loss of items sent, or damage of an item by the delivery carrier. Find a delivery carrier that you can rely on, and don't assume that cheaper is better. Remember, too, to claim for any lost or damaged goods.

Always take extra care with postage and packaging, and consider how appropriately your goods have been packaged. Most makers and craftspeople today are committed to using sustainable packaging, but there still needs to be sufficient packaging to protect items in transit.

Most delivery carriers offer a quick turnaround on compensation for lost or damaged items, so where possible refund your customer as soon as you're alerted and pick it up with the delivery carrier straight away.

Customer relationship management

Customer relationship management, or CRM, might sound like a complex infrastructure solely for corporations or larger brands, but companies of any size can develop an effective system for managing customer relationships.

CRM systems are set up to help companies better understand the correlation between sales and marketing efforts; some systems will combine this with inventory, shipping and possibly your accounts. These data management systems can give you powerful insights into how your customers are interacting with you, your products, your marketing and more.

WHO ARE YOUR CUSTOMERS?

Some small businesses work with off-the-shelf CRM products such as **Salesforce**. If you don't want to invest in software, you can create your own system by setting up a simple spreadsheet of contacts or a database. Also consider any other tools that you are using (e.g. Mailchimp) where you are already collecting customer data. When handling customer data it is really important that you understand your obligation to keep that information confidential. Mailchimp and other email newsletter software will often guide you through the steps of good data management, ensuring that customers can opt out of communications and prompting you to be careful of data when exporting.

In the UK and Europe, small businesses are governed by **GDPR (General Data Protection Regulation)**, which regulates the way that consumer data is handled. The key thing is to be clear with customers how data is handled once you have their names and addresses. As a business owner you have a clear obligation to protect their personal data and ensure that it is collected by you only for the purpose of a sale or booking, and that you will not pass on that data to anyone else. You also have an obligation to ensure that you store that data safely, so if you download data to pass on to third parties (e.g. to a bookkeeper or accountant), be sure that personal data is not shared at the same time.

CUSTOMER FEEDBACK

One of the quickest ways to get customer feedback is to send an alert some weeks after the sale of your product, or delivery of your workshop, and ask them to leave a review. There are also a couple of applications that can do this automatically – **Trustpilot** and **Judge.me**.

When dealing with a happy customer, remember to ask them to leave a review. One of the frustrating things about online reviews is that happy customers are sadly much less likely to leave a review than an unhappy customer. When you do get a good review be sure to shout about this as much as possible. Use customer testimonials throughout your site and on social media, as this all adds to your 'social proof' and acts as a powerful trust signal for your business.

Getting a bad review can be very demoralizing, but you have to simply take the feedback and learn from it. Always remain polite and start any response by thanking the customer for giving their feedback. As a small business owner it's hard not to take criticism very personally, but you have to try, where possible, to develop a bit of a thick skin as your business grows.

As you grow, you might also want to use surveys to get additional feedback on your products or services. You can use free surveying tools to conduct small surveys and find out how your products are being received. There are surveying tools you can use in **Instagram Stories**, or use **Typeform**, **Google Forms** or **SurveyMonkey** to get more in-depth responses from your customers to help you inform your future products or services.

On bad days, a great tonic for seeing any upsetting customer feedback is to go to the Instagram feed **@smallbizmemez** which is contributed to by a lot of independent maker businesses around the world. Once you start to see some of the things that a customer might give a business a one-star review for, it starts to put everything into perspective.

Exercise

1. Create a refunds and returns policy – there's a template available in The Making a Living Programme.
2. Do some further reading on customer statutory rights.
3. Consider how you can start to collate customer feedback.

10

Scaling Your Crafts or Maker Business

As your business grows, you may start to see patterns in your sales and your customers, or discover new ways of monetizing your work, and it's at this point that you may look to scale your business for growth.

Scaling your business is about taking things to the next level. It can create additional work and, of course, additional stress, so being clear about your goals and what you aim to achieve, and understanding what you will need to scale, will help you in this next stage.

Scaling is also about understanding whether you have hit a certain threshold and that you might need to reconfigure your business slightly to make it more scalable. This might include using materials that are more readily available, working with partners to create certain parts of your products, or employing other makers to create more products for you. All of these elements will create additional work streams for you so before scaling try to anticipate what these might be.

For example, scaling a business might entail:

- *hiring additional staff* – which means additional contracts as well as additional financial accounting, payroll and tax administration;
- *buying in materials at scale* – which might mean raising additional finance to pay for them before you have sold more products;
- *mailing out a much larger number of products each month* – which might entail new postage and packaging costs as well as more customer services;
- *new marketing strategies* – selling more products to more customers might entail bigger marketing campaigns, and this in turn might require upfront financing or additional staff.

Preparing to grow

For many companies, scaling for growth is often about getting the systems in place that will allow them to automate everyday tasks as much as possible and reducing the points at which human interaction is needed, so that they can cope more seamlessly if the number of customers, products and so on starts to grow rapidly. Scaling is about considering your current capacity and acknowledging whether or not your current systems could cope with growth – if not, then there might be a bit of work to do on infrastructure first.

One of the pitfalls of growing a business is that often it's only at the point of growth inflection that a small business owner realizes that their systems are not adequate for scaling. This might be when you start to see complaints about customer services, shipping delays or other flagged issues. It's at this point that you might want to take a step back and look at what needs to be changed in order to scale, and also to ask yourself the important questions, such as 'Do I want to scale?'

Harriet Vine

Harriet Vine is co-founder and creative director of Tatty Devine, now an internationally renowned jewellery business that has pioneered laser-cut jewellery since 1999. Here she shares her scaling journey and the challenges she encountered.

How did Tatty Devine grow in the beginning?

Tatty Devine started in 1999. We started on a market stall – totally word of mouth; there was no internet or social media or even smartphones!

Was there a point at which you sat down and considered a strategy for growth?

In 2006 we became a limited company, and a little while later, while working with Selfridges, we grew considerably both in number and in turnover – but this was not a good move. I think it is important to work out what success is for you – it is not necessarily financial, therefore growth might be better measured artistically or sustainably.

When looking at your products, did you see that some products or ranges were going to be more easily scalable than others?

Absolutely, we do two collections a year that are limited and completely free artistically, and then we have several smaller drops through the year with collaborators and other products that are more classic.

Did you need to raise additional finance before growing your business?

No, we found leather sample books on the street then spent the money we made on the market on a new sheet of leather. We were both students, no money, no responsibilities, so we had nothing to lose. A few years later we borrowed money from the bank to buy a laser cutter; it took seven years to pay back but it was the best thing we did – we have four machines now! The repayments on the machine were less than we were spending on laser cutting.

What were the biggest challenges when growing Tatty Devine?

Growing Tatty Devine has been over the course of 20 years; it has been slow and fast at times. Many things were a challenge. Getting our first team member was great but also made me question what my role was, as she came to make jewellery – which had been done entirely by myself up until then. Staffing, cash flow, how to manage wholesale clients – all off which require focus and development – come over time. You just really do have to learn something new every day.

What would your top tips be to other creative businesses considering scaling up?
Pricing, pricing and pricing. Make sure you add in the time it takes to make things. If you don't, you will never be able to pay someone to help you make them, and then a major pitfall would be never having enough time to develop new things, and eventually everything can become a bit stale. Make sure you love what you do and listen to your customers. They are the most important thing.

The exciting thing is that, with the right systems in place and the will to succeed, you can grow and scale your business. But scaling is not without its challenges, and you will need to consider the following:

- planning
- finance
- systems
- processes
- human resources (HR)
- selling wholesale
- specialist incubators.

We'll look at each in turn.

Planning

In your planning stage, it's really important to revisit your purpose and ensure that scaling your business is in line with your original mission, vision and values. Scaling might mean having to consider shipping or packaging that is not sustainable. Or it might be that, because you are buying materials in bulk, you are less clear on what impact shipping those materials will involve. Or it may just be the realization that the work/life balance you pledged to live might have to go on hold for a time. Before you do anything else, be clear on where you are willing to make adjustments for growth and the principles by which you stand.

At the planning stage, you will also need to start forecasting your sales, in order to try to understand the rate at which you are likely to grow and consider the points at which changes need to be made.

There are different levers that will help you scale and grow your business, including:

- growing the number of customers;
- growing the number of times they buy from your store (frequency);
- growing the amount of money that they spend in your store (average order value).

Creating a sales growth forecast or sales acquisition plan doesn't need to be complicated. If your e-commerce store is running off Shopify, for example, then finding the right data will be easily found in 'Reports' on your dashboard.

Exercise

Create a simple spreadsheet and plot out, using the knowledge of where your business is today, how you might grow:

- the number of new customers
- the number of orders
- the value of customer orders.

There is a template in The Making a Living Programme to help you with this.

Once you have some of these numbers in your spreadsheet, look at what impact these numbers are going to have on the rest of your business. If you're growing to 100 new customers a month, what impact will this have on you or your team? If you're growing your orders to 1000 a month, what impact will this have on your shipping costs, logistics and so on? If your revenue is starting to go up, what implications does this have for tax thresholds in your country? If you're suddenly handling a lot of stock, do you need bigger premises? The devil is in the detail, so try to map out each possible cost against a growth in sales.

Finance

As you start to map out your growth plans, you might start to see a gap between monies going out (for new expenses, infrastructure, software licences, etc.) and monies coming back in from sales. It's at this point that you might have to consider raising finance or borrowing money to bridge the gap.

If the idea of sitting down with your bank manager and asking for a business loan sends shivers down your spine, or just watching *Dragons' Den* (in the UK) or *Shark Tank* (in the USA) makes you come out in a cold sweat, then raising finance might not be for you. If you're putting in your own funds to grow your business, this is often referred to as 'bootstrapping'. The only complication with bootstrapping is that it means very different things to different people. For the ex-investment banker who has decided to scale their side-hustle creative business, 'bootstrapping' might actually mean some significant and meaningful capital is already ready to help them grow. If you can't meet the gap in your growth plan, you might need to consider raising finance yourself.

When you start to break things down and demystify some of the terminology, raising finance will just seem common sense. Can you convince someone that you are in a good position to be able to pay them back, or deliver them a return of investment? If you have the documentation to demonstrate your growth plan and how you would deliver it, and if you can show in a spreadsheet how an injection of cash is going to help you grow, then raising finance to fuel your business growth should be possible.

There are a number of other ways to help you scale and grow your craft or maker business that may not require raising finance.

Systems

The good news for small businesses today is that there are more and more amazing technology products coming onto the market that can help you to scale your business simply by investing in new software. Important software (some of which we have already mentioned in earlier chapters) that you might want to invest in includes:

- CRM (customer relationship management):
  - Salesforce
  - Glew
- email marketing newsletter builder:
  - Mailchimp
  - Klaviyo
- accounting software:
  - Xero
  - QuickBooks
- e-commerce store:
  - Shopify
  - Squarespace

Once these systems are set up properly, they can transform your business, automate everyday tasks and make it more scalable, enabling you to grow. However, getting these systems to talk to each other can cause confusion and stress, especially if you're not very technically minded. Finding that crucial contractor or freelance who can help you get the system that works best for you up and running is a worthwhile investment.

Remember that, with each of these systems, personal data that you are handling on behalf of your customers might be passing through, so be vigilant that your systems are protecting that data across any set-up.

Processes

Once your systems are in place, you will still need to set up efficient processes to ensure the smooth running of your business. For example, even if you use an accounting system such as Xero, you might want to consider paying for a bookkeeper to ensure that everything is matching up properly.

Human resources (HR)

Even with automated systems there are still going to be points during your business growth that you will need to hire additional staff. In the next chapter we will cover off employing people in more detail. If you haven't managed a team before then you should speak to other small businesses and get your head around what it means to be an employer. In the next chapter we'll look in more detail at the implications of growing a team.

Selling wholesale

As the global marketplace for handmade goods grows, so too do a number of wholesale businesses designed to make it easier for individuals to sell their handmade goods wholesale. These include Faire, founded in 2017, which is on a mission to 'help independent entrepreneurs chase their dreams, from the artisan candlemaker hoping to grow her business to the enterprising shopkeeper stocking his shelves with unique goods for his community' (*Source*: faire.com). The business model is helping small business owners to sell wholesale online.

When working with retailers looking for wholesale products you need to be clear that you understand the financial terms and logistics, as well as details such as returns policies.

Selling wholesale also requires you to price your product high enough initially to be able to let the wholesaler buy at a discount of your normal RRP. As we learned earlier from Sarah Marks (Chapter 2: Getting Started), 'If you are interested in wholesale, you need to price your product high enough at the outset to be able to still make a profit yourself. Wholesale normally means you sell your product to a shop at 30–50 per cent below the retail price.'

Specialist incubators

If the thought of scaling your business is daunting, you might want to consider going through a specialist incubator or a local small business incubator.

Incubators will offer subsidized programmes for small businesses and help them ensure that they have the pieces in place to scale. They are often supported by philanthropic organizations, government-led business initiatives or universities.

David Crump

In the UK, Cockpit Arts is a specialist organization working with craft businesses and individual makers at different levels – upporting start-ups taking their first steps and helping both mid-career and established businesses to accelerate growth.

David Crump, Head of Business Incubation at Cockpit Arts, explains a bit more about how the organization helps businesses scale:

What do you look for when you take on a new maker at Cockpit Arts?

We take people at any stage of their career. Through some of our Awards programmes, we do take on some makers who are not quite pre-start but certainly start-ups, and that's something we've been expanding. Our 'Make It' is specifically targeted at those who know they have a certain skill but haven't figured out if this could be a business. We are also looking specifically for people who are not generally represented in crafts.

So you're looking to grow diverse candidates from different socio-economic backgrounds?

Yes, we're especially looking for candidates where they live or come from a community where craft isn't a career that's looked at – it's our objective to increase that diversity. We take on makers at different stages, and we understand their skillsets might vary, but we are looking for a high level of craft skill. It might be embryonic with someone who is younger, but the raw talent is still there. We're also looking for a creative vision, both for their work and for their practice. Where am I trying to get to with this? Then, finally, we are looking for candidates with appetite and an understanding that they will need to work on the business side to grow it.

Are your makers working on the business full-time?
No, our makers often have other jobs. We're looking for them to be committed enough. Typically, if they're not going to do at least two or three days a week in the studio, then that's not enough to get enough momentum to take off. Sometimes they'll have a plan. Most of the people that join us each year, join through one of our Awards programmes. So, those Awards typically will subsidize their space or even pay for the whole space for the year, giving them the space needed for that take-off.

Could you describe a typical Awards programme?
One of our biggest funders is the Leathersellers' Company. We have a hub in Deptford [south-east London] with equipment provided by them, and they also subsidize places for up to three years and then the support tapers off. In the first year, they're paying your studio for you; by the third year, they're just giving you £1000 towards the studio. So it kind of softens the blow and makes it less of a cliff edge.

So the programme gives them the time and tools to be able to operate on their own?
Yes, but it's also a recognition that for most young people a year doesn't give them the time to get it off the ground. Unless they are already up and trading successfully, the chances are that they'll struggle to achieve the cliff-edge funding by the end of the first year. So, increasingly with funders, we're talking about support for two years and three years. The typical time for a business to really get off the ground in craft is four to seven years.

So you try to get them to think about long-term planning?
Yes, so you have a sense of what you're trying to achieve because you can meander, and suddenly, four or five years have gone past.

You're doing enough to be respectable, but actually you're not doing enough to move it to the next level.

What are the methodologies that you would use to help individual businesses realize their goals? Do you use visualization and affirmations?

Yes, Awardees that join us all go through a programme, and most makers when they first join us go through an end-to-end programme that starts off with the visualization process. Once we've helped them to identify a five-year vision, we break it down into goals for the next year and make SMART goals [SMART goals are: *Specific, Measurable, Attainable, Relevant* and *Time-bound*]. We use physical timeline planning, get the activities down, break down their goals and plot them into a realistic timeline.

How do you help makers scale?

At the scaling point, we're looking for blockages rather than goals and getting them to ask, 'What's stopping me in attaining my goals?' This is more like one-to-one coaching, and these issues typically centre on capacity and constraints that are stopping them from selling more. It normally falls into one of two areas – physical making restrictions or, on the business side, capacity or skills.

What are the common challenges for makers and scaling?

It really depends on what discipline they're in and what works. Weavers are a really good example because they can only go so far by hand weaving, and that takes you into a very definite price bracket. So, if they want to start wholesaling, they really need to outsource, and then there's a whole aspect about financially planning that. It's a big step.

What are the complexities of scaling if you are moving into wholesale or trade?

We run a series of financial workshops with makers to help them kind of think about what the impacts and implications of scaling are. The moment you're outsourcing, the need to be able to do a cash flow forecast is super critical. Another part of that equation is real and perceived value. So a big part of this is getting makers to look, not from the standpoint of their passion for what they made, but from the customer's point of view of what it is they're buying when they buy something from a craftsperson or maker.

One of the challenges for craft businesses is how reliant makers are on their hands because they're physically making everything. For some makers they are keen to explore what a growth plan might look like, while others just say, 'Actually, no, I'm just going to keep going and then one day I'll stop.' And that's that.

Do you have businesses serving both a high-end luxury customer and a more mainstream one?
Yes, so for handmade goods, there is a classic open studio customer who's buying something they see as quite rare and precious. On the manufactured side, you'll be going through wholesale, selling it through Heal's or Liberty [London-based upmarket stores], and so on. Some makers have been really effective at scaling up and evolving to become the designer, without doing any making anymore – but the perceived value is still there.

Is there a point at which a designer risks tipping too far into the mainstream?
They might tip into the mainstream, but whether that's too far or not is purely subjective. Typically, if they've managed to scale, then they're quite happy with the fact that that business has grown and they're doing well. If you can make that work, why not?

Exercise

Consider the following:

1. What are your motivations for scaling?
2. Have you identified what you are willing to forsake in order to scale?
3. Is designing more important to you than the actual making?
4. Are there upfront costs involved in scaling your business?

11

Creating a Team

As your crafts or making business grows, the likelihood is that you will need to start taking on extra resources and taking on an employee brings with it new responsibilities and complexities.

Taking on extra resources can really help you concentrate on other tasks and boost your own productivity. The best way to approach growing a team is not just to think about it as a way of handing over specific tasks, but to approach it as a way of building your brand with a committed group of like-minded people, who will support you and be passionate about the products or services you offer.

Before you dive in with growing a team, it's a good idea to get your head around HR legislation and understand the basics of being a responsible employer.

Being a responsible employer feeds into so many other elements of your business – finance, tax, legal and accounting – so it is imperative that you get it right. Your team, and the way that you treat your employees, is an extension of your brand values, and you will want to ensure that the way you grow your team is aligned with your purpose, your standards and your responsibilities.

When you start a business, understanding the peaks and troughs of your annual income and expenditure is unknown or, at best, erratic. So, before you rush into taking on full-time, year-round employees, take a step back to understand where you need support and when. Being realistic with your cash flow and managing expectations as you employ people is much easier than letting people go, which is one of the toughest processes for any employer to contemplate.

There are a growing number of people who have chosen to have a portfolio career today, so if you need a marketing expert but you really only need them one day a week for now, then that is what you should be looking for. As a first step ensure that you have your employers' liability insurance in place. Then read through this chapter carefully to help you to make better decisions and avoid pitfalls when it comes to growing your team.

Employing people – the basics

'What do I need help with?' This is your first question. To clarify, this is not the same question as 'What do I *want* help with?' We would all probably like a personal assistant to drop off our kids and take our clothes to the dry cleaners. Be realistic about what you need and where there are significant and risky gaps in your own knowledge or time. For example, if your finances are a mess and the thought of bookkeeping makes you want to go and stick your head in the sand, then consider either employing a bookkeeper or doing a basic accounting course and get on top of it.

A rough equation to use is to give yourself a day rate for the business and calculate how long it will take you to complete a task. If it works out cheaper to get someone in who can complete that task in a quarter of the time, then this is a wise investment.

For example, you need to reconcile a whole quarter of Shopify payments on Xero but you can't work out how to upload the right csv file, and how to surface the fees you have to pay on Shopify. You calculate your own day rate at £350 per day and that it would take you a week to work it out, and you know that you'd still be worried it was wrong. Or you have a bookkeeper who charges £175 per day, can complete the work in two days and will ensure that everything is completely aligned. In this instance it makes complete sense to employ someone with the right skills.

Another careful consideration is around social media and the resources needed to keep accounts up to date. Remember that creating endless digital content for social media is a bottomless pit – no amount of social media content is going to plug that hole. What might be a better use of your resources is to hire someone who is excellent at social media strategy who can help you to devise a content schedule that ensures that your social channels are regularly updated, but understands what is realistic for you to manage within your week instead.

Compliance with HR legislation is absolutely essential, but you also don't want the process to create lots of additional work for you. Getting the basics in place early on will help ensure that you are on the right side of your new responsibilities as an employer. Get your head around employee statutory requirements so that you are aware of your duties and the implications that this might have on your business.

Also, it's important that you understand the different types of employment status that exist in your country. Employees, freelancers and casual workers are all very different. There is a myriad of terms for employees, and it's important that you understand the differences, as your responsibilities as an employee will vary depending on their status.

Each country has its own terminology, but you can check online to ensure that you understand the implications of a way a role has been set up. In the UK consult https://www.gov.uk/employment-status.

In the UK, HMRC has a lot of information online, including a handy tool that helps you to ascertain if what you're proposing is for an employee or a casual worker, and explains the responsibilities of the employer in each scenario. HMRC can also explain the new IR35 tax law, which has impacted heavily on freelance consultants working through a limited company umbrella.

Get it in writing

The best thing you can do is to ensure that any agreements that you have with any employee are put into writing. This doesn't have to be a lengthy contractual agreement or entail legal fees, but could be a simple agreement or MOU (memorandum of understanding), signed by both parties, ideally *before* they come on board.

In this agreement you want to ensure that you include:

- your name as the employer, with your business address;
- the employee's name and their address;
- a job description with a brief outline of their duties and responsibilities;
- the date that the employment will begin;

- what they will be paid – remember to be clear how this will be taxed (e.g. at source through payroll), or if they're responsible for their own tax (e.g. if they are on a freelance contract). NB: Many consultants will be VAT-registered in the UK, so be clear on whether expected fees paid are VAT inclusive or exclusive;
- dates that employee will be paid – and clarification if they will need to invoice each month (for freelancers) and, if so, how soon they would be paid on receipt of invoice;
- where they will be expected to work;
- working hours, flagging any unusual hours (e.g. weekends for markets);
- terms and conditions including sick pay, holiday pay and pension;
- period of employment;
- notice period to be given if either party wants to terminate the contract;
- whether the employee is expected to work on their own computer or will be provided with a business one (when you've worked on your own computer for so long, you may well forget that employees will be expecting a computer to be provided). Also consider whether employees will be willing to use their own mobile phones for work, as this is not a given either.

You might also want to refer to any processes that you have in place around disciplinary rules or grievance procedures, and if the employee is going to be handling any confidential information, then be absolutely clear in the agreement the rules around confidentiality. You may also want to include a line about intellectual property, so be clear on things like designs created on behalf of the brand by an employee or contractor, so there is no doubt about the ownership of these if that person leaves.

If you have more than one employee at your company, then draw a clear line on how they will be managed and by whom – that is, who they should report to and when.

As a small business you're probably very used to just getting on with it, but for a new employee understanding how they check in with their work and know that their work is being done correctly will be really important, especially during the induction period.

Paying employees (and tax and pensions)

Outsourcing payroll to an accountant or bookkeeper can save a lot of administrative time and anxiety. Your goal as an employer is that all employees are paid correctly and on time, with the correct amount of tax and pension contributions taken off. A specialist will also be able to alert you to any shift changes in legislation and help you with queries to tax bodies like HMRC.

In the UK, all small businesses need to pay an employee's pension contributions – even for micro businesses. Your accountant should be able to help set this up for you and ensure that it is clear to both you and your employee. Once you have a pension scheme in place, you might want separate documentation that explains who the provider is and the processes of accessing that pension if they move on to other employment.

Remember that, with casual workers and freelances, you must pay the minimum wages required by your country's law.

Creating an employee handbook

If you're employing one person, you might think that an employee handbook is over the top, but just having a reference of your company's overriding principles and policies will help you and any future employee with a reference point regarding 'company rules'.

An employee handbook would normally come as part of an induction process that helps your new employee to understand health and safety procedures, data protection rules, dress code, working hours, code of conduct, the procedure for reporting sickness, and so on. If your new employee is going to be working in an office or studio, ensure that induction includes a full tour, information on any training on your systems, and introductions to others in the building.

If you know you're going to be frantically busy when they start, then be clear with them how and when they should ask you questions so that they don't feel completely isolated at the beginning. If your employee is going to be creating visuals for you, then this handbook might also include a brand style guide detailing fonts, colours and so on.

Hiring the right people

Finding the right people to join your team can be a challenge. Any new person joining the team is going to be an extension of you and your brand, and you will want this person to be a positive ambassador for you and your work. Finding good people is unusually hard. Many small businesses will initially hire friends or family members who they already know or close personal recommendations through their immediate network. Throwing the net wider may feel like a step into the unknown.

Hiring someone you know might feel like an easier option but you should still apply the same processes that you would for someone you don't know. Having a written agreement will ensure that everyone understands the terms, and an induction process will ensure that they understand their role and responsibilities. Having something in writing will save any misunderstandings later on and give you a reference to refer back to in case of any disputes. Remember disputes can still arise between friends and family members, too.

In the UK you're not legally required to advertise a job, but there are advantages if you do. When hiring, you should give careful consideration to getting the job description right and consider all aspects of the role. Have you been clear on any specific skills needed and made it clear what the responsibilities are?

Employers have a duty to ensure that employment procedures are not discriminatory, so check the job description thoroughly to ensure that your wording supports diversity and inclusion. Whatever the size of your team, pursuing a policy of hiring in an inclusive way will bring benefits to your organization. Ensure that when you write your job description that you surface it as widely as possible, and actively seek out candidates from different backgrounds.

In many countries it is against the law for an employer to discriminate on grounds of age, race, sex, marriage, disability, sexual orientation or religion. Ensure that your job description does not include requirements that might exclude people from applying.

When hiring, you need to ensure that you are on the right side of any necessary checks such as your potential employee's right to work in your country, whether they have a criminal record, and have a police clearance certificate such as that provided in the UK by the Disclosure and Barring Service (DBS). The last is especially important as you may need to make sure they are allowed to work with children, particularly if you host public workshops or work at festivals. You can also request references from previous employers before making a final decision about employing them.

Finally, be clear on whether your arrangement is a freelance contract or could be deemed to be employment, as your obligations as an employer will change accordingly.

Letting employees know how they are getting on

You might think that appraisals and performance management are just for big corporations, but all employees need to know where they are at and whether the job they are doing is good or not. Make the job description as clear as possible, as revisiting this regularly will allow both you and the employee to ensure that the role is continuing as described.

It is also important for any employee to understand what your goals are, so that there is a shared understanding of your vision for the company. Work together to set realistic targets – for example: 'Create a suite of templates for social media within the next two weeks'. Interim goal-setting will help employees feel they are moving forwards, even where the workload might be administrative or very varied.

Also, ask employees to let you know about anything that might improve their work or help them achieve it more easily. For example, it might be that an employee knows that having Photoshop is going to vastly improve their work, but unless they are given a platform to share this, you might never know.

Emma Sibley

Emma Sibley from London Terrariums gave us her experience of growing her business:

My first employee was one of my good friends. She could see I was struggling by myself and also she needed a job, so she pretty much said, 'I am coming to work with you.' This was the push I needed to grow the team and the perfect introduction to having an employee. When Iris left me two years later, I knew I had to rehire at least one more person to help me out.

When hiring for our team it's always funny as not many people have 'terrarium maker' on their CV, but knowing the skills needed, this is what we looked for – creative, an eye for detail and mainly being a welcoming and friendly part of the team. London Terrariums has been going for six years, and only now have I managed to delegate the two main avenues of the business – the workshops and the terrarium orders. Doing this has enabled me to grow the business in more ways than just the team; it's allowed us to expand our stores as well as the products we can offer and we cannot wait to keep growing!

The following templates are available in The Making a Living Programme:

- an employee handbook
- a job description
- a basic memorandum of understanding (MOU).

12

Legal Requirements and Intellectual Property

> **Disclaimer:** This chapter does not offer legal advice but considers some of your main legal responsibilities as a small business owner. Laws vary from country to country, state to state, and between industries, and we would always recommend that you take local legal advice to understand the rules that apply to your business.

Getting on the right side of your legal obligations as a business owner should be a priority and not something that you can kick into the long grass. As a small business, you simply cannot afford to ignore your legal responsibilities.

You will sleep much better and your business will be able to grow much more easily with some solid foundations in place, including setting into motion a commitment to good governance and ensuring that your business and practices are adhering to legal requirements.

The good news is that getting a framework in place to ensure that your business is compliant is not complicated, and for anything that does become a bit more complicated there are many legal firms that offer ad hoc legal services that don't always need to break the bank.

Paying out for some legal services at the beginning of your business journey can also save you a lot of time, stress and possibly money in the long run. One way to look at it is that these structures are put in place to protect your business as far as possible, as long as you are complying with the legislation and regulations.

Business Companion is an excellent UK government-backed site that has very helpful resources about trading standards: https://www.businesscompanion.info/

When you start a business you should check through the following:

1 BUSINESS REGISTRATION

Ensure that your business is correctly registered. As we discovered in Chapter 2: Getting Started, you need to make sure that your business is registered in the correct category depending on your set-up. Here's a recap:

- *sole trader / sole proprietorship* – where an individual has exclusive ownership of a business and is liable for losses;
- *limited company* – a private company whose owners are legally responsible for its debts only to the extent of the amount of capital they have invested;
- *limited liability partnership* – a separate legal entity from its members (partners), who are liable only for the amount of money they have invested, plus any personal guarantees. The partnership is incorporated and can be used only by profit-making businesses;
- *partnership* – an association of two or more people as partners, who share the management and profits of a business.

2 LICENCES, PERMITS AND REGISTRATIONS

Depending on what you sell or the materials that you use, your business might require a licence, permit or registration.

The kinds of craft or maker businesses that require a licence might be those that intersect with food or alcohol – so, for example, you might make ceramics which are then teamed up with a vinegar-making kit. You might also be working with hazardous materials or substances that require a licence to work with. Ensure that you do a thorough check to ensure that the way you work is compliant with your local authority or state law.

The possibilities are many, so make sure you research thoroughly what you need to do to be compliant with the law in your area, perhaps with the help of your local council or authority. Your city or county's business licencing agency is also a good place to start.

3 EMPLOYER OBLIGATIONS

When you become an employer you will need to be compliant with employment law. We covered a lot of these obligations in the previous chapter, as this is an important area and tied up with other employer responsibilities. Some of these obligations are connected to finances, such as PAYE, tax and so forth, which your accountant can help you with. You might want to invest in specialist HR support for anything more complicated.

To recap, your legal obligations as an employer centre on:

- equal opportunities
- employees' rights
- DBS checks
- written statement of employment
- national minimum wage
- pensions.

4 TAX

As explored in Chapter 8: Managing Your Accounts and Tax, the sooner you can start to get your head around taxation laws the better. If you opt to register as a limited company, you will need to pay annual corporation tax and as you hit certain thresholds you will have to register for VAT. If you're registered as a sole trader, you will need to register for self-assessment.

One thing to note is that tax departments do have actual humans working for them! If you're concerned about any tax implications, then make use of the customer services that they provide to get clarity, or, if necessary, sometimes a payment extension. Sometimes just picking up the phone or getting onto the online chat services can help you to clarify a complex question.

If you do need to register for VAT, ensure that you're clear on the quarterly deadlines for paperwork, as you may incur penalties if you don't get your paperwork in on time. If the thought of getting your tax wrong makes your stomach turn, then invest in a good accountant who can ensure that your paperwork is up to date.

In the UK, visit HMRC for more information: https://www.gov.uk/government/organisations/hm-revenue-custom

In the US, visit the Internal Revenue Service: https://www.irs.gov

5 INSURANCE

There are two insurances that are essential for small crafts or maker businesses – **public liability insurance** and **employers' liability insurance**. Many insurers now offer competitive packages for small businesses and will combine these two insurances into one policy. If you're a member of any major craft bodies you might find that public liability insurance is available as part of a membership package with some competitive rates.

If you're booked for public events, you will often be asked for a copy of your public liability insurance so be sure to have it at hand. If you work with particularly dangerous tools or materials in public spaces, then do always check with your insurer that your activity is covered.

Most insurance policies such as public liability or professional indemnity will help to protect your business from potential compensation claims, so ensuring that you are properly covered is a necessity.

6 HEALTH AND SAFETY

Safety for yourself and others is crucial, and businesses of all sizes should ensure that they have considered any risks are mitigated through planning. This responsibility extends to the public, employees and visitors. You must carry out a risk assessment, and on identifying health and safety risks, you have a responsibility to mitigate these risks to the best of your ability.

Regulations will differ depending on where you live, but consider who in your network can ensure that you are being compliant. For example, if you work in a managed studio, you can ask them for advice on health and safety within the building that you can then share with your employees and place in your employee handbook.

For many crafts and maker businesses there is a lot of interaction with different tools, many of which would be categorized as high risk. But it's not just the spoon-carving knives you need to worry about, a nasty paper cut at a school event can cause as much anxiety if you haven't considered the risks involved.

In studio spaces you may find that there are already some good frameworks in place to ensure that you have thought of everything. Some common mistakes, often small things overlooked, might include:

- *trip hazards* – are there wires on the floor or other trip hazards in the workplace or at the event?

- *portable appliance testing (PAT)* – have all the electrical goods that you're working with been PAT-tested so you know that they are safe to use?

- *temporary structures* – are there any temporary structures, at a market stall or fair for example, that are not sufficiently secured?

These are just examples, but the best approach is to do a risk assessment at any place where you or your employees are going to be stationed, even if just temporarily.

You should also consider that there might be specific health and safety legislation that is relevant to a craft or making technique that you use. For example:

- *stained glass* – you must check safety regulations controlling the use of lead;

- *upholstered furniture* – ensure that you check regulations around fire resistance;

- *kiln use* – check that your set-up complies with electrical and gas safety regulations.

In some workplaces there might be a dedicated member of staff who can offer medical support. If not, then consider the availability of first-aid kits and an accident book, giving a clear procedure for accidents or incidents that everyone understands – for example what to do if a fire breaks out. Some buildings will require you to have a safety procedure document printed out and placed in a visible area. Ensure that you understand the legal requirements and that your business is compliant.

If you have five employees or more in the UK, you are required to have a **written risk assessment**. A risk assessment broken down is about considering what might happen in a specific set-up and ensuring that you have considered the response in that situation.

Note that if you are doing any work that intersects with the public, or have been asked to bring workshops at a live public event. then you may be required to supply a risk assessment, so it's worth getting your head around what the questions and answers format of a risk assessment looks like.

It sounds obvious but often health and safety issues simply arise because of lack of tidiness. It could be a box that could be tripped over or a 'daisy-chain' connection of electric wires that creates an incident. Try to encourage a clean desk or workstation area policy as well as a clean studio policy so that your environment is a safe environment.

Take particular care if visitors come into your studio as, while you might be very used to dangerous equipment, they might not be. Before visitors come into a studio, always alert them to anything that they should not touch and any possible hazards.

7 ENVIRONMENTAL HAZARDS

If you're working with any hazardous products, ensure that you're clear on how these should be removed. Check whether your waste might be classified as hazardous – are you working with chemicals, for example? – and, if so, make sure that you know how to safely store and dispose of this waste. Most local authorities will have an authorized waste service that enables you to collect, recycle and dispose of hazardous waste.

8 PRIVACY POLICY AND DATA PROTECTION

A privacy policy allows you to specify what your business does with the personal data that it handles. We have already covered in Chapter 9: Customer Relations how important it is to handle customer data with care. In the UK this is a legal obligation dictated by the GDPR and Data Protection Act (UK). These legal requirements oblige you to work within the guidelines of how your customer and employee data are used, stored and processed.

Privacy policies and disclaimers limit your responsibility as a business in the event of something going wrong, so it's important to have these in place and visible on your website and in your terms and conditions.

One common mistake with data protection in crafts or maker businesses is how you capture customer emails at a live event or crafts market. Avoid asking customers to join a mailing list by writing their name and email address into a long list of other people's visible names and email addresses. Instead set up a simple sign-up form on a laptop or iPad, or a QR code, so that customers know that their data is being protected.

Another key area for data protection is email marketing. Understand what the law states for your country or state, and ensure that your email recipients are able to opt out of marketing emails and that customers are not automatically signed up to marketing emails without permission. Any email newsletters should have a clear **unsubscribe** option if customers wish to opt out.

9 DOCUMENTATION

Try to get into the habit of keeping your documents in place. When you're running a small business it can be easy to lose track of documents, so getting into the habit of filing documents around legal and financial matters will keep you in good stead for any future events. Even if you just have a 'dump' folder for documents, then at least you won't lose them. A common mistake is downloading a document and then clearing your downloads. Get into the habit of safely storing:

- financial documentation
- tax documentation
- expenses
- payments in and out
- employee contracts
- confidentiality agreements.

In many countries it is now a legal requirement to have a digital record of your finances, so get on top of your accounting software and make sure you understand how to reconcile your transactions coming in and out. If you need support, paying a good bookkeeper is a very worthwhile investment, which in the long run will save you money and anxiety levels.

Intellectual property

As a creative business you have a responsibility to ensure that you are not breaching any other business's intellectual property (IP). At the same time, you may want to put in extra measures to protect your own intellectual property.

Crafting and making by hand invariably create one-off products, but that doesn't mean that you shouldn't have an idea of which parts of your business, and your ideas, can be protected from copying by competitors.

Intellectual property is often referred to as 'IP' and enables businesses to protect:

- names of your products and brand;
- your designs;
- your inventions (if applicable);
- your written work, or photography and video content that you create.

Your rights to protect your intellectual property are protected by intellectual property law, which aims to help creators prevent their creative work from being copied or exploited. If you take the steps to register your intellectual property through the correct government organizations, then this will help you take action in the event of someone attempting to copy your ideas.

The main types of intellectual property are trademarks, patents, copyright and registered design rights.

TRADEMARKS
A trademark can be used to protect words, slogans, names, design, symbols and images. You can register your brand name or a product range as a trademark, and once approved you can add a ™ symbol to your branding to demonstrate that it is registered.

Trademarks can help you protect your brand name or logo from being easily copied. You can register your company name, your logos, your domain names and more. If someone then tries to use your trademarked brand name or logo, you can take legal action.

You also need to consider where you are registering your trademark, as you can protect yourself in your own country, or choose to pay an additional fee to protect your trademark in other countries, too.

Even if you don't register your trademark, you have *some* protection, and other businesses will not be able to trade under your name and 'pass off' their business under your trademark. You will always, however, be more protected if you register any trademarks properly.

PATENTS

A patent protects your inventions and can enable you to prevent others from making, using or selling copies of your invention without your permission. Patents are more regularly used in technology and industrial product design, but if you have a product that you think might be categorized as an invention, check with your government service. Patents are typically valid for 20 years and need to be filed in *each country* where protection is wanted.

If you have devised a specific way of processing your product, you might want to consider protecting your methodology through patent protection.

COPYRIGHT

A copyright protects original works by an artist or author. Copyright can help creators to protect their artwork, work of literature, piece of music, photograph or craft work. In the UK, creative works are protected under the Copyright, Designs and Patents Act 1998, in which the most relevant category for us here is the 'artistic work', which can include any 'work of artistic craftsmanship'.

To be protected by copyright law, work must be deemed 'original', and a 'degree of labour, skill or judgement' must have gone into creating it. The work must have actually been created; an idea alone is not enough.

Copyright protects all original works, but the issue with crafts and making is that there are many makers and craftspeople using similar techniques and the possibility of creating similar works is likely, so proving the originality of work can prove difficult. If you have developed a particularly distinctive style, you might want to consider registering a copyright to protect your work.

REGISTERED DESIGN RIGHTS

Registered design rights are also relevant to makers and craftspeople as they enable businesses to protect others from copying the appearance of a product or design. When registering designs they must be new at the time and have an individual character. This protection might include appearance or physical shape or the way it is configured.

As with all legal matters, you should seek professional advice, as legal frameworks differ between country to country and it is important that you protect yourself within the legislation that is designed to protect you and your work specifically.

You can find more information on this tricky area from the following organizations and websites:

- Intellectual Property Office (UK) – www.ipo.gov.uk
- The Patent Office – www.patent.gov.uk/index.htm
- Design and Artists Copyright Society (DACS) – www.dacs.org.uk
- The Copyright Licensing Agency Ltd – www.cla.co.uk
- The World Intellectual Property Organization – www.intellectual-property.gov.uk
- US Copyright Office – www.copyright.gov/help/faq/faq-general.html
- United States Patent and Trademark Office – www.uspto.gov

Legal obligations checklist

- *Right structure:* How is your business set up and are you registered correctly?
- *Tax:* Do you understand your tax obligations and have you anticipated when these might change? Do you need to register for VAT?
- *Health and safety:* Are you clear on your responsibilities as an employer around health and safety?
- *Licencing:* Do you need any specific licences to sell your products or services?

- *Business insurance:* Do you have adequate insurance in place – employers' and public liability?
- *Intellectual property protection:* Have you considered how to protect your ideas, product ranges or branding?
- *Employer obligations:* Are you clear on your legal obligations as an employer?
- *Privacy policy:* Do you have an adequate privacy policy in place, and do you make it clear to your customers how you will protect their data?
- *Documentation:* Do you have systems in place to enable you to document important information relating to your business?

13

How to be a Responsible Business

Being a responsible business is simply about putting the pieces in place to ensure that you can grow your business with due care and consideration, and take full responsibility for your company's actions and its impact on any employees, stakeholders, the wider community and the environment.

As a business owner you will have learned that you're *legally* responsible to implement a number of key actions to ensure that you are running a baseline responsible business. Complying with statutory law, however, is just the beginning, and there is a new movement growing around the world as more and more business owners go the extra mile to create a world where business can balance profit and purpose and work for social good.

Responsible businesses will have specific standards about the way they conduct their business, how they treat employees, how they might reduce their impact on the environment, how they might support diversity in the workplace, and so on.

Leading this charge is the **B Corporation** (B Corp) movement, which is helping to develop new kinds of businesses that balance purpose and profit. This might mean that businesses work to ensure that their decisions have a positive impact on their workers, customers, suppliers, community, and the environment. Some B Corp members are small businesses while some are multinationals.

Many maker and craft businesses are aligned with the principles of 'responsible business', and there are some simple actions that you can take to establish a responsible business framework to work within, without creating lots of additional work. In fact, running a responsible business is 'good for business', with a growing number of customers looking for ethical and sustainable brands to support, and a generation of potential employees who want to work for responsible brands that look after their employees.

There are a number of recognized certified processes available, including B Corp certification, that can create an additional trust signal for conscious consumers. By looking at such processes you might be able to get some good pointers on how you can improve your business as you grow – from changing your bank account to improving your supply chain.

This checklist will help you to consider some of the key things you can do to ensure your business can grow responsibly:

1 Create a code of ethics

Although as a business you don't legally have to have a code of ethics in place, having these documents in place as you grow your business will help to ensure that your company culture is retained even as you scale. A code of ethics might include statements on issues such as ethics, values, environmental policy, diversity, employee respect and customer service.

2 Protect your employees

As we've seen in the chapter on growing a team, having the right systems in place will ensure that you protect your employees and keep them safe and well. There are also legal requirements about protecting your employees.

3 Follow sustainable practices

More and more craft and maker businesses are on a mission to ensure that their businesses are being run with the environment in mind, looking to see how their work feeds into the circular economy and ensuring that their supply chains, too, are following sustainable practices. What are the policies and practices that allow your business to monitor your environmental impact? From the materials in your products to the packaging you use, consider how you can hone and improve your practices.

Katie Treggiden

Sometimes the process of improving and implementing these practices can feel overwhelming, especially if you're a small creative business. Journalist, author and podcaster **Katie Treggiden** had observed that 'sustainability' is such a broad term as to have become almost meaningless, and prefers instead to focus on the circular economy.

Katie has created a simple circular economy framework that is especially geared for designer-makers. This translates the three tenets of the circular economy, as defined by the Elle MacArthur Foundation, into actionable steps and mindsets for implementing them. The visual device in Figure 13.1 maps out these actionable steps and mindsets.

Figure 13.1 The circular economy framework
(courtesy of Katie Treggiden)

Katie explains: 'Making design circular is about embracing waste as a raw material, considering repair in everything you create and thinking more like nature. Each of those three approaches comes with three mindsets or approaches that will help you to integrate them into your business.'

Katie's three approaches to sustainable crafts are:

1. *Use waste*. Waste can be unpredictable and inconsistent, so an experimental approach is vital. Collaborating with others can mean working with a company to utilize its waste streams, learning from makers two steps ahead of you, or partnering up with someone to split the process of turning waste into materials and then products between you. Finally, it's important that you let the materials dictate the design, listening and learning to what they can do rather than forcing them into predetermined forms and functions.

2. *Repair.* The first principle of repair is to design with its end of life in mind – that is, to consider how your product will be broken, repaired and even disassembled at the end of its life before you even put it out into the world. When repairing, it is important to respect the stories and cultures of both the object you are fixing and the repair techniques you use – the power of storytelling is an exciting part of repair culture, when we remember whom those stories belong to. And finally, when the function of an object cannot be restored, think about what else it could do and keep its materials in use by including 'repurpose' in your definition of repair.

3. *Think like nature.* Last but not least, we must stop thinking of ourselves as separate from the natural world. We are part of nature. Think about bio-fabrication and how you might be able to collaborate with nature to grow rather than make. Move beyond the notion of doing less harm, and instead think about how your creative practice can nourish the environment. And finally, ensure that everything you create can be disassembled and go back into the earth in a way that reintegrates with natural systems to their benefit.

4 Be aware of the supply chain related to materials

One of the hardest things about being a responsible business is understanding where materials *really* come from. You might buy materials from a supplier, but you might not know where they source materials from. Following the supply chain to source can sometimes be hard to monitor, but many companies are now calling for more transparency so that they can be sure that all parties in the supply chain, for example, have been paid and treated fairly.

Charlie Bradley Ross

Charlie Bradley Ross is founder and director of Offset Warehouse and the Sustainable Fashion Collective. Here she shares her top tips on ensuring that your supply chain is ethical. Charlie explains:

> When we're talking about 'ethics' we mean the environmental and social impacts of a product. The environment includes any adverse effects on the environment, such as the chemicals flushed into the local waterways, unsustainable raw material production, air pollution, destruction of biodiversity, and so on. The social impact is broader, as it not only includes the people who work in the supply chain directly creating the product, but also includes animal welfare and the impact on the customers of those products.

To help you navigate the issues around the supply chain, Charlie has provided some quick tips on things to consider when choosing a supplier. Choose a supplier that:

- empowers communities and creates jobs;
- allows trade unions;
- considers energy consumption and uses natural resources, including sunlight, wind and rain;
- minimizes waste;
- restricts, contains, cleans or reuses any hazardous waste run-off;
- uses sustainable water systems;
- provides safe and clean working conditions;
- does not operate forced labour conditions;

- pays above minimum wage, if not the living wage;
- does not enforce excessive working hours;
- does not work with unaudited or 'invisible' subcontractors;
- does not discriminate against their workforce;
- prohibits physical abuse or discipline;
- offers access to affordable childcare or a facility on the premises;
- advocates for national governments to write and act out good labour laws;
- implements educational and training programs in the work-place.

In addition to the above, consider low-impact raw materials and choose those that:

- are made from materials that replenish quickly, are recycled or recyclable to the same quality (and not downgraded);
- improve biodiversity;
- require low energy and water to make;
- do not require hazardous chemicals to produce.

Although this list might seem overwhelming, checking a company's own website and seeing their statements on labour and sustainability may help you quickly get a picture of your suppliers' approaches to sustainable and responsible business practices.

5 Work with charities or consider donations

Align yourself with charities or fundraisers that represent your values or share your vision. For example, BEEN London makes bags out of recycled materials. It has partnered with non-profit organization Tree Nation to enable it to plant a tree every time a bag is bought. There are also a number of initiatives now that help businesses to make contributions to support environmental organizations such as 1% for the Planet.

Exercise

1. Create a code of ethics.
2. Create a plan outlining how you might improve your company's sustainable practices.
3. Investigate your supply chain.

14

Wellbeing and Resilience

Running your own business will be challenging. There will be times when you feel invincible and like you're winning, and times when you just want to curl up in a ball or go back to your old office job. Keeping a tab on your wellbeing is not a 'nice to have'; it is absolutely crucial to growing your business without falling over.

Managing your time

If you're used to working for someone else, then you might find that clocking off is much easier working for someone else's business, in comparison to your own. There is so much to do that the temptation to just keep working into the evenings and weekends will be strong. Aim, however, to create some boundaries between yourself and your business during the week.

Downing tools for a period of time will help you and your business, allowing you to come back refreshed and rejuvenated to fight another day. Create a healthy work/life balance from the outset and try to stick to it. Of course, there will be busier times of the year, such as winter markets, where you might have to work longer hours, but look to mitigate these busy periods with some quieter periods to preserve your wellbeing.

At the beginning of each day try to focus on the one task that is going to really help propel the business forward that day. It's too easy with all the distractions of email, social media, family and more to be pulled in various directions, but by identifying first thing in the day what your most important tasks are you will be able to focus and move the business forward.

If you're running your own business, there is a strong chance that you will have 101 micro tasks that you could be doing, but this is obviously not going to be realistic in a day. Learn to prioritize and focus on the tasks that are most important and will be most effective. Ideally, write down your three top tasks to tackle in a day and relentlessly focus on those. Many people find techniques such as the Pomodoro technique useful, which encourages you to focus on specific tasks within a time frame and take regular breaks in-between but in short bursts.

Keeping things in perspective

There will always be bad days. A bad day could be a market where you don't sell a single product, a customer who complains about something they've bought, or a company that cancels what would have been a well-paid workshop at the last minute. Dust yourself off and take stock of the situation, learn the lessons, and see whether you can improve your own systems to ensure that these things don't happen again.

As a business owner you will need to learn how to build up your resilience and keep things in perspective.

Miranda West, publisher at the creative entrepreneurship publisher The Do Book Company, offered this advice on perspective, speaking at the Do Lectures in 2015:

> 'Because (the business) is your thing, it can become all-consuming and you think about it when you go to bed, and you think about it when you wake up. I remember thinking I'm going to have to manage this. One way that I found to do this was to literally go somewhere, I would go to a physical place like the sea or a church, somewhere much bigger than me and gradually that sense of scale would come back.'

Setting realistic targets

Ambition is great, but realistic interim goals will help to keep you motivated and ensure that you know you're moving forward. If you're having a month where everything feels stagnant, take the time to look at how far you've come and identify milestones that will help you feel like you are achieving your goals.

If you have worked on your mission, vision and values, look to measure the impact of your work so far. Not all impact is measured in monetary terms – it might be that you have helped 30 children to learn a new skill as part of a creative programme, or that your work has inspired someone enough for them to shout about how great you are on Instagram. Celebrate the small wins and use these as rocket fuel to drive you forward.

Identifying distractions

We all have distractions but some of them really eat into our potential working time in the week. Try to identify what these distractions are and consider some strategies to help you avoid them. Perhaps the most common distractions are:

- mobile phones
- social media
- email.

MOBILE PHONES

Mobile phones are designed to distract you – fact! Most applications are designed to pull you back again and again, especially social media applications. If you can, keep your mobile phone in another room while you work. We all have numerous excuses for why we can't do this – 'What if the school calls?', 'What if there's an emergency?', 'I need my phone to verify applications on my desktop', and so on.

Carve out some times in the day when you can check your mobile phone or have it on your desk at a time when you know you'll need it for something like a two-step verification (or, better still, create a two-step verification on your desktop). If you're really worried about not being contactable for more than a few hours, then at the very least turn off your notifications, which are simply designed to get you back down the rabbit hole.

SOCIAL MEDIA

This is obviously linked to mobile phones, too, but social media can create huge distractions for small businesses. Identify what is 'social media for work' and what is scrolling through competitors' websites and wondering how they got as far as they did (clue: probably by not spending too much time on social media). Social media can also cause individuals to lose focus: you might see a competitor and think, 'Why aren't I doing a reel?', for example, when if you actually focused on your own business goals and concentrated on the actions that will move your business forward, then you might realize that dancing in front of the camera is not necessarily the right thing to move your own business forward.

EMAIL

Email is a strange one, as it's easy to think that opportunity might come in an email, and many worry that they are going to miss out if there is not an immediate response. The truth is that many of us treat our inbox like our 'to do' list, so whoever is shouting the loudest via email gets your attention. Structure your day so that you write down your priorities for the day *before* you open your email, and you'll start to notice that your priorities do not necessarily match the priorities of the person at the top of your inbox. As we saw in the chapter on customer relationship management, getting back to customers promptly *is* important, but if you can attempt to carve out some dedicated times of the day when you look at email you'll start to see how much time you can get back to doing the things that are most important to your business.

Acquiring the habits of successful entrepreneurs

Hal Elrod, author of *The Miracle Morning: The Not-so-obvious Secret Guaranteed to Transform Your Life Before 8AM,* has developed a routine called SAVERS after speaking to several successful entrepreneurs about the habits they felt contributed to their success. He collated the best of these and devised 'SAVERS', which stands for 'Silence, Affirmations, Visualization, Exercise, Reading and Scribing' – a 'Miracle Morning' routine to help you focus your day. You don't have to be a spiritual person to use these, and you may find that they really help you to focus and make each day count. You can go much more deeply into any one of these in the book, but, broken down simply, the routine involves:

- *Silence* Find just five minutes or more to quieten the mind before starting your day. You might think that the morning is the worst time of day to find five minutes of silence, but consider setting your alarm to go off before your kids get up; alternatively, find the five-minute window that will work for your timetable.

- *Affirmations* Positive affirmations are a simple way to encourage yourself that *you* can do this. Write down some simple affirmations that remind you that you're 100 per cent capable of meeting the challenge of running your own business and say these out loud in the morning and, ideally, before you go to bed, too. There will be days that you say these affirmations out loud through gritted teeth, but they do help!

- *Visualization* Use a private Pinterest board or other photographic pinboard to visualize your goals. Seeing is believing. Be ambitious and learn to really visualize what success looks like to you.

- *Exercise* Get out of the house every morning if you can and do a short run, walk, yoga session or anything else that gets your body moving, ideally outdoors. Exercise is known to support wellbeing and will help you focus throughout the day.

- *Reading* Learn from the many entrepreneurs who have come before you. Make use of their mistakes and pitfalls and learn as much as you can from them. Also, read fiction to take you away from the day-to-day and use it as a way of switching off at the end of each day.

- *Scribing* Scribing is simply about writing down the things you are grateful for. In the thick of it you will forget all the good things in your life, and writing down regularly the things and people in your life that you are grateful for will help your wellbeing and help to keep your work in perspective.

These are just examples, but you might want to create your own bespoke morning routine that works for you and is achievable for your specific circumstances or home set-up. The aim of a daily mindset routine is simply to put you in the best possible mental state to achieve your goals that day.

PRIORITIZING YOUR TIME

Learning to say no is a key business skill in itself. Sometimes things present themselves that look like a fantastic opportunity but, once analysed, they are clearly a liability. As a first step, learn to say 'I'll think about it', rather than accepting an invitation straight away.

If someone wants to meet up to discuss something, consider if it has to be next week. What really works for your work schedule and can you group together meetings in an afternoon so that you have a section of the day that is interruption-free?

Consider your own goals and design your own 'decision tree' to help you think more clearly when opportunities arise.

SLEEP

A good night's sleep will help you mentally and physically with the tasks of growing a new business. If you find that you're getting tired during the day due to lack of sleep (if you have young children, for example), then embracing the daytime power nap is an amazingly effective way to help you recharge your energy and get back to your desk with renewed focus.

MARIE KONDO YOUR DESK

Having a clear desk policy will reduce the risk of distraction and encourage focus. Taking just five minutes to declutter your desk is an effective way to break up tasks during the day and will help you to focus when you sit back down again.

EMBRACING AUTOMATION

Learn to love robots and let them do the work for you. My own mother, a professional maker, used to put the washing machine and dishwasher on in the morning and say, 'Right, I've got the staff on it.' Today we have a suite of very sophisticated automated services at our fingertips, from automated emails to automated accounting, from automated sales communications to automated customer services, and more. Find out which tools can help your business with automated tasks.

Developing a peer-to-peer network

Talking to other like-minded businesses will help you see that you're often sharing the same challenges. Tap into any local networks or global networks of makers and craftspeople who are in the same online marketplaces as you and share your experiences, and pick up tips to help you grow your business. You can also use free tools such as Slack to create your own specialist network and engage with your peers on the things that matter most to your business. You'll be amazed at how willing others are to share their experiences and how generous people are in trying to help.

Sophie Nathan

Sophie Nathan is an artist, maker and accredited creative coach based in London. Here she shares her top tips on how to create resilient strategies, overcome setbacks and relieve stress, so that your small creative business can really flourish and thrive.

1. *Find connection.* Cultivate a love of the outdoors and nature, from local parks to woodlands, to really connect yourself back to things bigger than yourself. This will help you gain perspective into where you are in your business and how best to overcome challenges.
2. *Just breathe.* Combine walking with moments of quiet solitude. Find a 'sit-spot' and for five minutes simply allow yourself to clear your mind and focus on your breath, breathing deeply as you sit there. Allowing this small amount of time to just let go

will do wonders for your creative mind and give you the space to allow clarity and vision back into your practice.

3. *Set yourself a challenge.* Challenge yourself to do a project that is slightly out of your comfort zone but has no business repercussions. Maybe you make jewellery, but love pottery as a pastime. Your challenge could be to throw a pot larger than you've ever thrown. It might take a few attempts to get there but, once you've mastered it, you'll build a new level of confidence for the other things you can achieve with your life and career.

4. *Find time for play.* Don't forget time for play. An improvisation class is a great way to push your limits, test your imagination, meet new people and, most importantly, have fun! Whether you're starting or maintaining a small creative business, it's too easy to forget making time to enjoy yourself. Remember that you got into this business to do the things you love – so make sure you are finding time for that.

5. *Get reflecting.* Try to find time each day to create a practice of writing through journaling. This writing can be 'free association' and mean nothing! Just sit down and set a timer for 15 minutes and start to scribble. Even if it's just 'I don't know what to write, I don't know what to write', try to keep going for the whole 15 minutes. You'll be amazed at what it uncovers and what it sets right.

These simple tips are designed to quickly uncover blockages that could be holding your business back, helping you to expand a product range or, most importantly, simply inject some fun back into it all!

Enjoying the journey

Sometimes we're so focused on reaching a goal that we forget to enjoy the journey. The likelihood is that you've decided to start a craft business because you believed that it would offer you a specific lifestyle. Relish in the aspects of your work which might seem like hard work but are actually an important part of running a craft or making business. Yes, it might be a pain to be unpacking the boot of your car at a market again, but try to relish in the camaraderie of the process and find some time for some conversation with other makers and craftspeople along the way.

Most important of all, remember how this whole journey started, acknowledge your love of making and creating again and again. Find the time to make and create for your pleasure only, so taking it away from creating stock for the business and towards creating purely for you and your own wellbeing.

As a maker or craftsperson, you've likely already learned that you need to appreciate imperfection as an essential part of the learning process of making. Building your crafts or maker business requires much the same approach and mindset. *Making a Living* has brought together the many interesting insights and lessons from businesses run by individuals just like you. It has been designed to give you a realistic picture of the process and offer practical advice to get your creative business off the ground.

There is no reason to not start growing your crafts business today, and be reassured that you are not alone. Join like-minded makers and craftspeople from all over the world in the online community, and share your own experiences of your journey in *making a living.*

Annexe: A guide to becoming more environmentally conscious in your craft practice

Become more environmentally conscious in your craft practice with this useful guide from the Green Crafts Initiative, including simple tips and advice on cutting down on waste, saving water and swapping your materials for more sustainable alternatives.

Together, Creative Carbon Scotland and Craft Scotland created the Green Crafts Initiative, a sister project to the Green Arts Initiative. The Green Crafts Initiative is a nationwide accreditation scheme designed to provide Scotland-based makers and craft organisations with the advice, support and the tools they need to become greener.

1. Collective buying sustainable materials

Often for makers, the biggest environmental impact of craft has already occurred at the point when one begins to work with the raw materials. As a result, choosing more eco-friendly materials, and working with more sustainable suppliers, is one of the biggest ways a maker can improve the sustainability of what they do.

However, sometimes sourcing more sustainable suppliers can incur a financial cost. Either in the time spent researching and experimenting with a new supplier, or in an increased cost in the material itself due to higher ethical or environmental standards.

To overcome this issue, it is possible to group together with other makers to either work with suppliers to leverage lower prices, or to take advantage of economy bulk purchasing.

THINGS TO LOOK FOR IN A SUPPLIER

Sustainable alternatives to your materials will vary depending on your discipline, and there are a few things to consider. For example, in ceramics, the availability and sustainability of a certain type of clay. In jewellery you might need to consider whether the mined precious stones are certified as non-conflict sourced.

Moreover, there are some things to examine when identifying whether a supplier is more sustainable than an alternative:

- Environmental policy: does the supplier have a positive stance on sustainability? Do they have a policy on their aims in this area? (normally in the About section, or the footer of supplier websites). Can you ask them about what they are doing to reduce their impact?

- Locality and seasonality: do they source locally to you? Can they do so for particular products? Do they know what is seasonally appropriate for your needs?

- Toxicity: do they have a process for controlling any toxic waste created from their production processes?

- Social dimensions: do they support their local community? Are they a social enterprise?

- Carbon reduction initiatives: do they offer anything like carbon-neutral delivery?

HOW TO ORGANISE

In order to seek and assess more sustainable (environmental and economic) buying options through a collective model, one needs to see what the available options are, and who would be likely to work with you. At a very simple scale, this could be working out who else buys from the same suppliers (is there a popular brand among your raw material suppliers?), or who else from your discipline is interested in investigating more sustainable options.

For example, collective purchasing to secure a better rate for energy supplies has been very popular in the past, and following a similar model on a studio or sector scale could be a good way to begin the process.

- Advertise: let others know you are looking into the sourcing of a particular material

- Register: get them to inform you of who their current suppliers are, what they are currently paying/using, and how much they tend to order on an annual/equivalent basis.

- Negotiate: talk to your selected suppliers about your sustainable materials option, using the leverage of the amount of business your collective may bring them.

- Switch: confirm and purchase the products at the agreed rate, and distribute to the new community.

2. Saving water in production

Water is one of our most crucial natural resources. However, due to the propensity for it to rain in Scotland, we Scots are notoriously bad at taking it for granted! Essential for human life and a huge range of domestic, industrial and craft purposes, our water supply needs a huge amount of movement and processing to make sure it's suitable for our needs.

There are lots of ways individuals and studios can reduce their water consumption and increase their resource efficiency – and lots of reasons why they should.

REASONS TO REDUCE YOUR WATER USAGE

Saving money, building business resilience and reducing impact on the environment are the key reasons to reduce your water usage. More specifically, for those who pay business rates for water, there are increasing costs around use and disposal, more pressure from government and regulators around safe water management, and more awareness of the carbon emissions impact of water use and its effect on climate change.

Ways to save water:

- Report leaks: even something as simple as a leaking tap wastes around 80 litres of water (enough to fill an average bath)

- Plug it: you can save two litres of water by using a plug in the sink when washing your hands

- Turn it off: only turning the water on intermittently when cleaning equipment saves around three litres of water
- Use it cold: use only cold water for cleaning floors or rinsing equipment

GETTING STARTED

Understand how you use water: considering how you use water in your processes and activities, where your biggest use of water is, and whether the water you use is heated/treated before you use it will give you a picture of your needs, and where you might be able to reduce your use.

Understand your bills: How do you pay for your water and do you receive a water bill? Comparing monthly or annual use, and understanding how this may correspond with your activity, will help you focus on cost reduction.

Consider new, efficient equipment: often new equipment can boost the efficiency of water use, offsetting the upfront cost of the equipment in a relatively short time frame. Some organisations may offer an interest free loan for new equipment that has resource efficiency savings (energy, water, waste). Some examples of such equipment might be:

- Tap aerators, which break up water flow into droplets for better wetting and reduced water use.
- A rainwater harvesting system for grey water use (e.g. toilets, cleaning).

3. Sustainable ceramics

Ceramics are the oldest form of technology humanity has, from cooking and storing food, to preserving and telling stories. Porcelain, stoneware and earthenware are just some of the major types of potteryware produced by heating natural materials (often clay) to remove water for thousands of uses, with everything from crockery to jewellery.

As well as being a popular craft form for individual makers, industrial ceramic production is also commonplace. Although the latter has more of a carbon footprint, this article focuses primarily on the choices and the changes makers can make to develop a more sustainable practice.

SOURCE MATERIALS: ORIGIN, TRANSPORT AND LOCALITY

Beginning with the core input materials for any ceramic creation, interrogating the sources of clays and glazes is a good first step.

CLAY

Clay is abundant in the world (some estimates indicate that everyone is no more than 200 miles from some clay), but it is still a finite resource that's extraction produces much pollution and habitat degradation. Like other raw materials (such as metals), some varieties are more popular or more available than others, and makers should strive to source clays that are not so rare as to make their mining process damaging to the natural environment.

Similarly, sourcing clay more locally will reduce the carbon emissions and environmental impact of the international transportation of clays. Although gathering your own clay may not be suitable for everyone, working in collaboration with businesses like brickworks (who may allow you to reclaim their offcuts) or mining from the excavation waste of quarries could root your practice more locally in the near environment.

Finally, being mindful of the opportunities for working with reclaimed clay, past unfired projects, and using offcuts for the production of slip are all ways makers could reduce the raw material intensity of this input.

GLAZES

There are a huge variety of glazes used by ceramicists in their work, each producing unique effects which are often central to each individual's practice. Generally, makers should aim to use non-toxic, non-harmful colourants, and seek to use more naturally-derived dyes. In particular, avoiding any colourants that contain heavy metals (like lead) is a priority: waste materials often end up in waterways as a pollutant.

A note on salt glaze: in the past, salt glazes have been of particular environmental concern due to their production of an acid by-product. However, in the context of wider environmental impact, energy and transport emissions are much larger and more significant, and this should likely be where efforts in the sector are concentrated.

PROCESSES: INCREASING EFFICIENCY

Once you have established greater sustainability in the materials you use, examining the form and efficiency of the firing process is a good next step.

Huge amounts of energy are required to heat a kiln to a suitable temperature, but it is possible to maximise the efficiency of that energy usage through a variety of methods.

STACKING AND SHELVING

Makers already adjust how they form and stack kilns to achieve particular effects and finishes, but experimenting with the density of stacking can ensure that the kiln is being used as efficiently as possible. Generally, the higher the density of the stacking, the higher the temperature required; but sometimes lower temperature firings have to be extended in time due to the thickness of the clay, which in turn could make them less efficient. As every maker's method (and kiln) is different, it's best to try and monitor these variables to see how you can create the best effect with the lowest temperature and shortest time.

STAGGERING KILN USE

For those working in ceramic studios, one technique to reduce energy use is to stagger the uses of kilns throughout the day to better spread the energy use in the building. If all studio kilns are turned on at the same time, then it artificially inflates the demand for energy from the national grid, which in turn drives national energy production. This is most classically represented through the phenomenon of TV Pickup, a term used to refer to a phenomenon that affects electricity generation and transmission networks.

Similarly, in small studios, group firings might be possible: combining multiple kiln firings into a single event significantly increases the efficiency of the energy use.

RESEARCHING AND ADJUSTING YOUR OWN KILN

Each kiln form (whether electric, wood etc.) will have a range of settings or methods of use to increase efficiency, and should be addressed on a case-by-case basis (through things like experimentation and manufacturers instructions – often the basic pre-programmed settings are not the most efficient).

- In many cases, wrapping kilns in ceramic fibre can massively improve their efficiency

- Adopting an industry-style firing time of around eight hours can also be a key way to reduce energy use by avoiding long pre-heats or overnight warm-ups

- Sometimes drying work with an electric fan, rather than using kiln re-heats, can be more efficient (depending on the kiln)

SUSTAINABLE AND ALTERNATIVE FUELS

Considering the energy supply to your kiln is also a way to make the firing process more sustainable. Changing your electricity supplier to a green tariff increases the demand and profile of renewable energy, and considering local materials when sourcing wood kindling or other fuel is a more sustainable approach. Recently the ability to use sustainably produced biodiesel or Waste Vegetable Oil (WVO – the kind produced by chip shops) in kilns instead of fossil fuels has created the opportunity to use biodegradable waste products for firing.

CERAMIC WASTE: THINKING CREATIVELY

Typically ceramics cannot be recycled through waste processing plants (household or industrial recycling). They can be downcycled (ground up and the powder used for slurry) but the result is often of a lower quality than the original. An alternative option is to creatively test if waste materials can be combined through a kiln casting process to form new materials (such as bricks, tiles, countertops). As well as being a potential income generation stream, this reduces the demand for virgin raw materials for these purposes.

COMMUNICATIONS: TALKING ABOUT GREEN ETHOS

One of the key ways makers can become more sustainable is by using their influence to reduce the environmental impact of their own practice, those they work with and that of their customers. Informing visitors to your website of your sustainability ethos and actions is a key way to drive change. All makers living and working in Scotland are also able to join the Green Crafts Initiative free of charge: a community of practice run by Craft Scotland and Creative Carbon Scotland that support and enables makers to reduce their environmental impact.

This extract is taken with kind permission from Craft Scotland and the Green Crafts Initiative.